Text by William Marvel

Additional text by Donald Pfanz

Maps by George Skoch

Thanks to the interpretive staff at Fredericksburg & Spotsylvania National Military Park. Special thanks to Robert Krick for invaluable assistance in completion of this project.

Published by Eastern National Park and Monument Association, copyright 1993.
Second printing, 1995.

Eastern National Park & Monument Association aids and promotes the historical, scientific and educational activities of the National Park Service. It also supports research, interpretation and conservation programs of the Service. As a nonprofit cooperating association recognized by Congress, it makes interpretive material available to park visitors and the general public.

*Cover:* The Irish Brigade presses toward Marye's Heights. Painting by Don Troiani. Photograph courtesy Historical Art Prints, Ltd., Southbury, Connecticut.

*Back cover:* Fredericksburg residents return to their shattered homes. Painting by David E. Henderson. (NPS)

# The Battle of Fredericksburg

As the night of November 7, 1862, passed inexorably into history, a howling Virginia blizzard buried more than 100,000 sleeping Union soldiers beneath their blankets. The storm hurled corn-sized kernels of snow against a glowing wall tent near Rectortown, where, by the light of a lantern, the commander of the Army of the Potomac scratched away at one of the long letters he was wont to send his wife each day.

At thirty-five, George Brinton McClellan was younger than many of the captains in his army, but he had worn the twin stars of a major general for a year and a half. The Federal host that sprawled across a hundred and fifty square miles of the Old Dominion represented the fruit of his personal labor, and most of the men under those snow-covered blankets had never known another leader. They had followed McClellan up the James River peninsula that spring, had glimpsed the very spires of Richmond with him, and when that campaign failed they had rejoined him in Maryland at the end of summer; under his cautious eye they had hammered the Confederates at Antietam on September 17.

GEORGE B. MCCLELLAN

(USAMHI)

Now—largely because he had not pounded the enemy quite so hard as he might have in that battle—he had begun shepherding his army down another road to Richmond.

A rap on the tentpole interrupted McClellan's letter and ended his career as a soldier. Two officers ducked under the canvas, their overcoats dusted in white, and after some courteous banter one of them produced an order relieving McClellan from command and supplanting him with the other visitor, Ambrose E. Burnside.

A major general like the man he replaced, the tall, bewhiskered Burnside had been friends with McClellan since their first days together at West Point, nearly two decades before. When the Panic of 1857 and a duplicitous secretary of war drove Burnside's firearms factory out of business, it was McClellan who had found him a job and offered him a place to live. McClellan had also probably recommended Burnside's original appointment as a brigadier general and had authorized his first independent command, an amphibious division with which Burnside secured the North Carolina sounds. For the past two months Burnside had been McClellan's senior subordinate (if not his closest one) and leader of the largest wing of the army. Burnside succeeded his friend reluctantly. Twice the previous summer President Lincoln had offered him the command and twice Burnside had refused, doubting that anyone but McClellan owned the organizational capacity to manage the largest army

AMBROSE E. BURNSIDE
(LC)

Burnside arranged an elaborate farewell ceremony for his old friend. Thousands of blue uniforms lined up in the fields near Warrenton on November 10, and in the brisk autumn air "Little Mac" cantered out of the war to volleys of cheering.

## THE STRATEGIC SITUATION

While the Army of the Potomac tipped its caps and banners to McClellan, bigwigs in Washington asked Burnside what he intended to do with his army, which stretched from Manassas Junction to Waterloo, more than twenty miles away. Burnside's immediate command consisted of the First, Second, Third, Fifth, Sixth, Ninth, and Eleventh corps, totaling 130,000 infantry, cavalry, and artillery. The Twelfth Corps, another fifteen thousand strong, stood detached at Harpers Ferry.

The smaller Confederate army lay scattered in an arc around the blue behemoth, like a wolfpack sizing up a herd of caribou. General Robert E. Lee had divided his Army of Northern Virginia into two wings under lieutenant generals. He had concentrated James Longstreet's corps of 38,000 at Culpeper Court House, fifteen miles south of Waterloo,

ever to walk the continent. McClellan, however, had become the target of Republican politicians who saw him as the standard-bearer of Democratic opposition to their radical aims, and his dilatory pace frustrated Lincoln's hopes for a quick end to the rebellion. By the end of the 1862 congressional elections the pressure to remove him had grown too great to resist. The president had determined to put another man at the head of his largest army—hopefully one who might cooperate more cordially—and in the end Burnside took the job rather than let it go to someone he considered less capable than himself.

Burnside introduced himself rather diffidently to his new subordinates, some of whom secretly resented his willingness to replace their hero and viewed his acceptance of the command as evidence that he had taken sides with the hated radicals. In deference to the great mutual affection between McClellan and the troops,

ROBERT E. LEE
(THE VALENTINE MUSEUM)

blocking the direct road to Richmond. Meanwhile Thomas J. Jackson, the legendary "Stonewall," held his 37,000 troops at Winchester and the gaps north and west of the Federals. Major General J. E. B. Stuart's eight thousand cavalry guarded the fords south of the Yankee army.

Henry W. Halleck, the general-in-chief of the United States Army, ventured down to the Warrenton Hotel with a couple of staff brigadiers to hear Burnside's plans. Conventional political wisdom still called for the capture of the opposing capital, Richmond, and Burnside's only alternatives were to march straight south, subsisting his army via the railroad, or to sidestep to the Tidewater, supplying himself by steamship at each of Virginia's navigable rivers. The Orange & Alexandria Railroad needed much repair and could probably not have satisfied the stomachs of so many men anyway, besides which it would have demanded substantial detachments to guard against raids. On the other hand, Union gunboats unquestionably controlled the water. Burnside therefore proposed marching swiftly to Falmouth, on the Rappahannock River, and crossing into Fredericksburg before Lee could oppose him. From there he could travel along the less vulnerable Richmond, Fredericksburg & Potomac Railroad until he reached the Pamunkey River, where he could advance from a new base of supply.

Halleck habitually avoided important decisions, and he did not like the plan, but he agreed to take it back to the president for his consideration. Burnside had learned that the Rappahannock bridges had been burned at Fredericksburg, so he also asked for a pontoon train with which to span the river. The army's pontoons all remained on the upper Potomac, where McClellan had crossed back into Virginia, but the Washington generals left Burnside with assurances that the bridge materials would be at Fredericksburg waiting for him: they predicted only three days for delivery.

While he awaited an answer, Burnside reorganized his unwieldy army. He joined the First and Sixth corps to form the Left Grand Division, putting it under William B. Franklin; the Third and Fifth corps became the Center Grand Division, commanded by Joseph Hooker, while the Second and Ninth corps constituted Burnside's Right Grand Division, under Edwin V. Sumner. He left the Twelfth Corps at Harpers Ferry and positioned the Eleventh Corps nearer Washington, as a reserve. Franklin, Hooker, and Sumner were all major generals, and all were older than Burnside: Sumner had already been an officer for five years when Burnside was born. With the exception of Sumner, none of them held Burnside in high regard. Hooker did not hesitate to criticize his commander, especially behind his back; many in the army and in Washington felt Hooker should have been the man to replace McClellan, and Hooker was one of those who thought so. These three were his most senior generals, though, and Burnside had little choice but to appoint them. He hoped, mostly, that the consolidation would ease confusion at headquarters.

## Burnside's Plan Approved, Then Foiled

When he returned to his comfortable office in Washington, Halleck did present

> *Hooker did not hesitate to criticize his commander, especially behind his back; many in the army and in Washington felt Hooker should have been the man to replace McClellan, and Hooker was one of those who thought so.*

Burnside's plan to Lincoln, who approved it with the caveat that Burnside would have to act quickly. Halleck did not attend so conscientiously to the pontoon question, however, and Sumner's troops stepped off toward Fredericksburg before the pontoons even started down from the upper Potomac. The first Federal infantry tramped into Falmouth on the evening of November 17, and General Sumner asked permission to cross some cavalry over a precarious ford to take Fredericksburg, which was lightly defended. Burnside declined, lest the horse soldiers find themselves trapped by rising water, and indeed rain began to fall as though on cue. Burnside ached to cross while the city was lightly defended, too, and when he rode into Falmouth on November 19 he wrote Halleck that he would do so as soon as the pontoons arrived.

The first of the pontoons did not even leave Washington until that day, and (because General Halleck had not apprised his engineer officer how badly Burnside needed them) they rolled out on ponderous wagons. The same storm that lifted the Rappahannock turned Virginia roads into muck, and the pontoon train slowed to a crawl, stopping altogether at the washed-out bridges over the Occoquan River. Only then did the engineer in charge of the work divert some of the pontoons to a steamboat, which delivered them at Belle Plains landing on November 22. Even these few, enough for a full bridge or two, did not reach the army until November 24. The bulk of the pontoon wagons finally pulled up at Falmouth, ready for use, on the afternoon of November 27—some ten days after Burnside expected them.

By then it was too late for the Army of the Potomac to waltz unchallenged into Fredericksburg. As early as November 15 Lee suspected that Burnside might be headed for Fredericksburg, and he sent a regiment of infantry and a battery of artillery to bolster the city's garrison. Lee

ALFRED WAUD SKETCHED THIS VIEW OF FREDERICKSBURG AS SEEN FROM FALMOUTH JUST DAYS BEFORE THE BATTLE.

(LC)

A TRAIN OF PONTOONS LIKE THOSE USED BY BURNSIDE TO SPAN THE RAPPAHANNOCK RIVER. THE TARDY ARRIVAL OF THE PONTOONS UPSET BURNSIDE'S PLANS FOR AN EASY CROSSING AND ULTIMATELY DOOMED HIS CAMPAIGN TO FAILURE.

(NA)

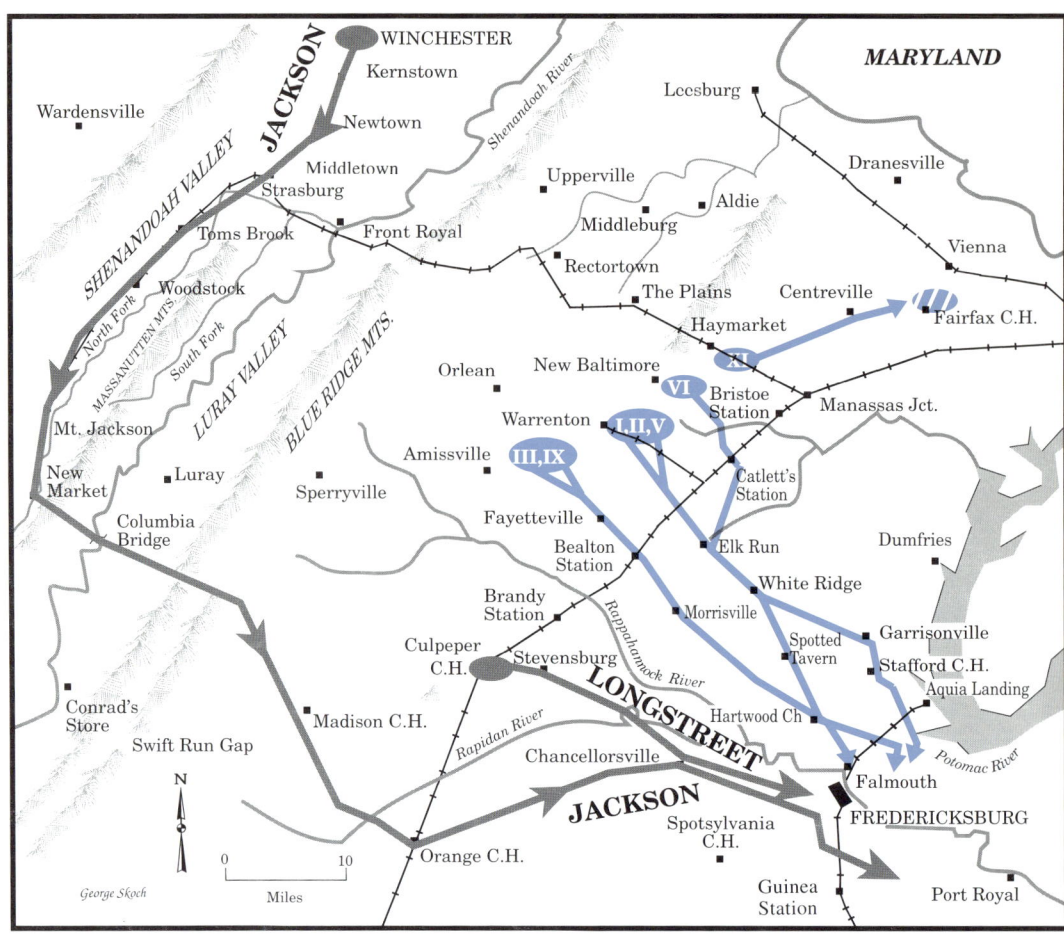

BELOW: AT THE TIME OF THE WAR, FREDERICKSBURG WAS A COMMERCIAL TOWN OF 5,000 INHABITANTS. WHEN CONFEDERATE FORCES ABANDONED THE TOWN IN APRIL, 1862, THEY DESTROYED THE BRIDGES ACROSS THE RAPPAHANNOCK RIVER.

*THE ARMIES MOVE TO FREDERICKSBURG, NOVEMBER 15-DECEMBER 4*
*When the Fredericksburg Campaign opens, the Army of the Potomac is centered near Warrenton Junction, north of the Rappahannock River. On November 15th, Sumner's grand division marches toward Fredericksburg, followed by Franklin and Hooker. Burnside plans to cross the Rappahannock River at Fredericksburg, but is prevented from doing so by the tardy arrival of his pontoon train. By the time the pontoons arrive, Longstreet's Confederate corps occupies the heights behind the town. In early December, Jackson's corps arrives from the Shenandoah Valley and takes position south of Fredericksburg, toward Port Royal. With Jackson's arrival, the Confederate army is reunited and ready for battle.*

thought, incorrectly, that Burnside favored shipping his army back to the James River. Consequently the Confederate commander supposed for a time that the Fredericksburg movement merely served as the screen for a general withdrawal back to the wharves at Alexandria. By the morning of November 18, however, he started two divisions of Longstreet's corps on the road to Fredericksburg, following it with the balance November 19. The next day Lee himself telegraphed Jefferson Davis from Fredericksburg to say he believed the Yankees were concentrating for a strike at that place. The last of Longstreet's corps filed into the city on November 23, and on that day Lee directed Stonewall Jackson to bring his corps east of the Blue Ridge Mountains.

In one of his messages to Jackson, Lee intimated that he did not intend to resist Burnside on the Rappahannock. The geography favored the Federals there, he felt, because of the heights that towered on Burnside's bank of the river. Lee preferred the North Anna River, where the high ground would have loomed on his side, but he probably guessed that his president would frown on retreating so much nearer to Richmond. Employing his renowned tact, he therefore tried to persuade Davis of the wisdom of a Fabian withdrawal, destroying the railroad and otherwise impeding Burnside's progress until winter; he posed the notion in such a fashion that Davis might feel it had been his own idea. Lee's diplomacy did not succeed, but neither did the Yankees offer to cross the Rappahannock immediately, so Longstreet's corps remained in camp on a long ridge a mile southwest of the river.

## Burnside's Second Plan

His advantage squandered by the pontoon fiasco, Burnside cast about for another plan. On November 26 he met with President Lincoln aboard a steamer in Aquia Creek. The commander-in-chief suggested moving the army downstream to Port Royal and crossing there. A separate force—an expedition Lincoln was fitting out in New York just then, under Nathaniel Banks—could simultaneously proceed up the Pamunkey and cut off Lee's retreat. Burnside argued that jockeying so many troops into place would consume too much time, putting the campaign too far into winter—just as Lee had proposed to his own chief executive. Ultimately General Halleck agreed with Burnside on that point, so Lincoln laid away his idea and General Banks took his troops to Louisiana, but the president told Burnside not to feel that he must be hasty about fighting his legions.

Burnside knew better, however. Judging from the public reaction to McClellan's indolence the previous year, he could hardly turn his troops into their winter quarters. Nor, after all the disheartening changes of base the army had already endured, could he move to another theater of operations—like the James River peninsula, where the cold and rain would impede him less. That would have discouraged soldiers and civilians alike, as General Lee fully realized. Burnside had but one option, and that was to push ahead on the line he had already taken before winter was too far advanced.

Faced with strong resistance at Fredericksburg, Burnside looked for another crossing more than a dozen miles downstream, at a place called Skinker's Neck.

*Burnside had but one option, and that was to push ahead on the line he had already taken before winter was too far advanced.*

The ground still lay to his advantage there, and the enemy had not yet thrown any force in his way, so Burnside began corduroying the roads to that more isolated location. Further rain had only worsened the clay Tidewater byways, and until Burnside could secure a landing on the opposite bank he would have to supply himself overland from Aquia Creek and Belle Plains. At the same time, engineers designed a line of entrenchments opposite Skinker's Neck. The preparations alerted Lee's pickets, however, and early in December Burnside detected the arrival of Confederate troops to cover that crossing, too. These Southerners proved to be the vanguard of Jackson's corps, for Lee had finally completed the concentration of his army.

## FREDERICKSBURG FINALLY TARGETED

EDWIN V. SUMNER (BL)

Stymied again, Burnside realized that he could not now make an uncontested crossing anywhere, so he decided to bridge the river where the enemy would least expect it—right in front of the city.

Despite Burnside's warning to evacuate the civilian population, Lee had expressed doubt that he would ever strike there, or that he would try to lay his pontoons anywhere between there and Port Royal because the banks were so difficult. In fact, Lee anticipated the very plan Lincoln had proposed, with Burnside landing at Port Royal under the protection of navy gunboats and marching to cut the Confederates off at Bowling Green while Banks's army (which Lee had learned of) struck up one of the rivers at Lee's back.

Jackson's earthworks at Skinker's Neck convinced Burnside that Lee had divided his army between there and Fredericksburg, and he supposed he might throw down his bridges quickly, step between the two halves, and defeat the enemy in detail. At the least, he could hope to confront Longstreet's corps before Jackson arrived to reinforce him.

Burnside's eldest and most devoted lieutenant, General Sumner, had proposed a radical plan to the commanding general. Citing the firepower the Confederates could converge on the bridgeheads from the city waterfront, Sumner thought the entire army could more easily cross on the plain below town if enough artillery were brought up to support it. Then Burnside could march around Lee's right flank by the main road, abandoning his own line of supply and forcing Lee to fall back and protect his. Fredericksburg might thus be taken with much less loss.

Sumner's design was a good one. He was not the only one to think of it, and Burnside apparently considered it for a time, but eventually he opted for a more complicated strategy that might not only keep Lee off guard but impede his escape. He would divide his forces, crossing Sumner's Right Grand Division into the city and Franklin's Left Grand Division onto the plain downstream, while keeping Hooker's Center Grand Division for a reserve. Franklin would hit the Confederate right at

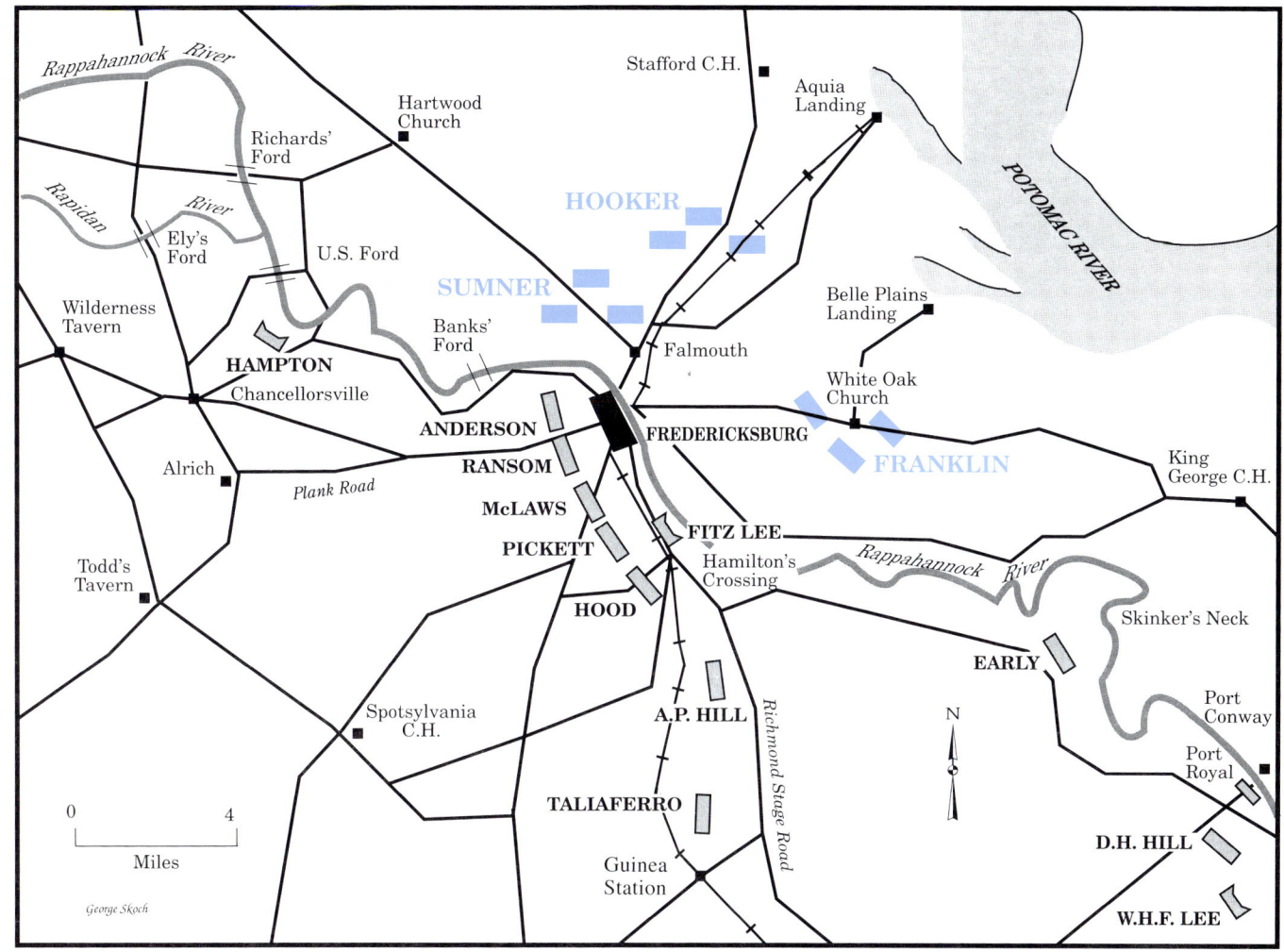

*BURNSIDE IS POISED TO CROSS THE RIVER: DECEMBER 10*
*Prior to crossing the river, Burnside masses his troops near Fredericksburg. Sumner's grand division is camped closest to town, near Falmouth; Franklin is three miles to the east, at White Oak Church; while Hooker's troops are in reserve, near Stafford Court House. On the Confederate side, Longstreet holds a seven-mile line stretching from the Rappahannock River above Fredericksburg to Hamilton's Crossing, below the town. Jackson's corps is scattered over a wide area between Hamilton's Crossing and Port Royal, while Stuart's cavalry guards the army's flanks.*

Hamilton's Crossing, and Sumner would assail the heights beyond Fredericksburg, forcing Longstreet to either stand and fight while Franklin flanked him or to retreat in the face of a direct onslaught. Not only would such an approach be more likely to dislodge Longstreet, it might throw his corps into a rout and lead to its capture, either in whole or part.

Burnside issued preliminary orders outlining his plan on December 9, and that evening General Sumner called his corps and division commanders together to familiarize them with the details. Major General Darius N. Couch, in charge of Sumner's Second Corps, said that most of the senior generals doubted the army would be able to cross in front of Fredericksburg; perhaps they shared Sumner's fear that forewarned Confederate infantry and artillery could annihilate any troops who crossed on bridges there.

# CHATHAM

Across the Rappahannock River from Fredericksburg, on the bluffs overlooking the town, stands Chatham, a plantation house built by William Fitzhugh beginning in 1768. At the time of the Civil War the house was owned by J. Horace Lacy, a major in the Confederate army.

Union troops occupied Chatham for the first time in April 1862, when General Irvin McDowell set up headquarters at the house. McDowell brought a corps of 30,000 men to Fredericksburg. He halted his command at Fredericksburg for a month in order to bring up supplies, after which he planned to march on Richmond. President Abraham Lincoln journeyed to Fredericksburg to confer with McDowell about the proposed movement and on May 23 dined with him at Chatham. That very day, Stonewall Jackson's Confederates attacked Union troops in the Shenandoah Valley and briefly threatened Washington, D.C. As a result of Jackson's success, Lincoln ordered McDowell to forgo his march on Richmond and take a portion of his command to the Valley instead. General Rufus King took over command at Fredericksburg in McDowell's absence and moved into Chatham.

The next prominent figure to come to Chatham was General Ambrose Burnside. The War Department summoned Burnside to Virginia in August to reinforce Union troops defending Washington. While waiting for his troops to debark at nearby Belle Plains, the genial, bewhiskered general camped on Chatham's front lawn. While there, he received a visit from his friend General George B. McClellan, whose troops, like Burnside's, were then steaming north on ships to protect the threatened capital.

On September 17 McClellan defeated Lee at Antietam, and the armies again drifted back to Virginia soil. Antietam was McClellan's last battle. Annoyed by the general's hostile attitude and frustrated by his unwillingness to bring Lee to battle, Lincoln ousted McClellan in November 1862 and appointed Burnside to command the Army of the Potomac in his place.

Burnside quickly took action. Within ten days after assuming command, he had his army marching east, toward Fredericksburg—and disaster. Leading the march was General Edwin V. Sumner, the 65-year-old commander of Burnside's Right Grand Division. Sumner reached Falmouth, opposite Fredericksburg, on November 17, but Burnside forbade him to cross the river without pontoon bridges, which did not arrive for another week. By then, Lee's army occupied the heights behind the town.

For three weeks Burnside delayed, pondering his options. When he finally tried to cross the river at Fredericksburg on December 11, Mississippi riflemen barred the way. Burnside wrathfully shelled the town and in the afternoon ferried troops across the water. The Mississippians held their ground until sunset, then fell back to the main Confederate line at Marye's Heights. By dark, Union engineers had bridged the river in several places with pontoons.

On December 12, Sumner's Right Grand Division filed past Chatham on its way to the bridges. The next day, with his army in place, Burnside attacked. William B. Franklin assailed the southern end of the Confederate line, while Sumner's men gallantly, but unsuccessfully, tried to storm Marye's Heights. Forbidden by Burnside to cross the river, Sumner watched the destruction of his command from Chatham's second-story porch.

CHATHAM: A WARTIME VIEW
(USAMHI)

A NEW JERSEY SOLDIER MADE THIS SKETCH OF CHATHAM WHILE CAMPED IN THE AREA.

(CUMBERLAND COUNTY, NEW JERSEY, HISTORICAL SOCIETY)

By the time the battle had ended, 1,200 Union soldiers were dead and another 9,500 had been injured. Many of the wounded soldiers received care at Chatham. Clara Barton assisted wounded soldiers at the house as did poet Walt Whitman, whose brother George was numbered among the casualties. For surgeons working in Chatham's north wing, amputation was the order of the day. Surgeons tossed mangled limbs out the window, and they landed at the foot of catalpa trees in the front yard. A huge pile of limbs accumulated there—about a load for a one-horse cart, Whitman noted. Patients who survived the ordeal were sent to general hospitals in the North. Those who did not were wrapped in woolen blankets and buried beneath Chatham's cold sod. At least three soldiers remain buried on the grounds to this day; the rest have since been interred at the Fredericksburg National Cemetery.

The Union army wintered in Stafford County after the Battle of Fredericksburg. Union pickets guarding the river cut down Chatham's trees and piled the wood in the downstairs fireplaces to keep warm. As the trees disappeared, they tore paneling from the building's interior for fuel and scrawled their names on its barren walls.

Meanwhile, the Army of the Potomac gained a new leader. In January 1863, Joe Hooker replaced Ambrose Burnside as the army's commander. Hooker led the army across the Rappahannock River above Fredericksburg in May and engaged Lee at Chancellorsville. At the same time, General John Sedgwick's Sixth Corps and John Gibbon's division of the Second Corps crossed the river at Fredericksburg and menaced the Confederates from the coast. Gibbon made his headquarters at Chatham—the last Union general to do so.

Sedgwick successfully attacked the Confederates at Marye's Heights, but later retreated across Scott's Ford when confronted by Confederates at Salem Church. Gibbon (whose division had remained in Fredericksburg) likewise withdrew, taking up the pontoons behind him. Once again Chatham became a scene of cruel suffering, as wounded soldiers—North and South alike—found care and shelter within its walls. When space on the dirty floors gave out, tents were erected on the grounds around the house.

By the time the war ended in 1865, Chatham was in desolation. The house's elegant interior had become a ruin; its beautiful grounds, a graveyard. The property languished until the 1920s when General and Mrs. Daniel Devore restored the house to its former splendor. Chatham's last owner, John Lee Pratt, donated the house to the National Park Service in 1975. Today it is the headquarters for Fredericksburg and Spotsylvania County National Military Park.

The next afternoon, December 10, Burnside chaired his own conference at the Lacy mansion, Chatham, with Sumner and the chief officers of the Second, Third, and Ninth corps. He said he planned to begin building the bridges before dawn the following day. Debate over the news rose immediately and lasted for hours. Burnside's subordinates apparently resisted him, challenging the wisdom of bridging the river there. Many of the men on Sumner's staff suspected that any crossing before the city would be attended with great slaughter, but the meeting appears to have ended with everyone agreeing to give the operation his best effort. From there Burnside rode away to brief Hooker and Franklin.

## THE BRIDGES

Well before dawn on December 11, engineers in sky-blue overcoats began wrestling the pontoons down the steep bluffs of Stafford Heights to the toe of the riverbank, launching them into the ice-encrusted water and fastening them together. The thumping and banging of the hollow boats echoed across the Rappahannock to the brick facades along Water Street, where Confederate marksmen lay, waiting and listening, with their rifles primed.

These Southern pickets lurking in cellars, parlors, and back bedrooms belonged to William Barksdale's Mississippi brigade. Barksdale allowed the construction to proceed for more than an hour, meanwhile posting about half of his brigade along the waterfront, but when the tandem bridges neared the midpoint of the stream he sent a courier back to Longstreet's main line to say that the enemy had committed himself. At about five o'clock a pair of Confederate cannon barked a warning of the Union advance, and in the gray predawn the Mississippians started popping away at the cottony shadows flitting back and forth on the fog-shrouded bridges. A hundred or so Floridians trotted up to join Barksdale's men, seeking out lairs from which they might help delay the crossing as long as possible.

The first rippling fire dropped a few carpenters of the 50th New York Engineers, including Captain Augustus Perkins, who may have been the first man killed in the battle; the rest of the crews darted back into the fog. Federal infantry answering the volley from the riverbank could not see through the thick mist, but under this ineffective cover the engineers eased back out to add a few more pontoons. Their mallets roused the sharpshooters again, and another

WILLIAM BARKSDALE'S MEN HELD BURNSIDE'S ARMY AT BAY THROUGHOUT DECEMBER 11 BY PREVENTING CONSTRUCTION OF BRIDGES AT THE MIDDLE AND UPPER CROSSING SITES.

(BL)

ragged rattle of musketry felled some of the foremost workmen. Back went their comrades, and Burnside sent half a dozen field batteries down to the riverbank to blast the marksmen out of their shelter. The big guns suffered from the same poor visibility that foiled the infantry, however, and within a few minutes of resuming their task the engineers had to run for safety again.

Several times the crews dashed out to complete the bridges—Confederates counted nine separate attempts—but nothing seemed to dislodge the snipers, and by ten o'clock fifty of the New Yorkers lay dead or wounded. The rest would not go out again, so the commander of the engineer brigade, Brigadier General Daniel P. Woodbury, gathered eighty infantrymen from Connecticut who were willing to give it a try. He double-quicked them toward the bridges with lumber on their shoulders, but the fog was thinning now and Mississippians picked off a few of them before they stepped on the first planks. The others threw down their tools and bolted back to their regiments.

Well downstream, at Franklin's crossing, the 15th New York Engineers had already completed a bridge, although some of Gen. Hood's men sallied out at the last moment and leveled a sharp fire for a few minutes. Six of the Yankees fell wounded, but their infantry escort drove the Mississippi skirmishers away and the final

UNION ENGINEERS ATTEMPTED TO THROW BRIDGES ACROSS THE RIVER WHILE UNDER FIRE. "I WAS GREATLY MORTIFIED IN THE MORNING TO FIND THAT THE PONTONIERS UNDER MY COMMAND WOULD NOT CONTINUE AT WORK UNTIL ACTUALLY SHOT DOWN," WROTE GENERAL DANIEL P. WOODBURY. "THE OFFICERS AND SOME OF THE MEN SHOWED A WILLINGNESS TO DO SO, BUT THE MAJORITY SEEMED TO THINK THEIR TASK A HOPELESS ONE. PERHAPS I WAS UNREASONABLE."

(LC)

planks dropped into place at nine o'clock. Alongside this bridge, a battalion of Regular Army engineers lagged a couple of hours behind the 15th New York. Confederate skirmishers likewise attacked these Regulars at about the same time, but the Southerners managed only to wound one carpenter and capture a couple of men who were grading the approaches on the far side before they, too, were discouraged by Union infantry supports. Once finished with the first span, the 15th New York helped the 50th New York to build a middle bridge at the lower end of town.

Burnside had hoped to see his infantry and artillery pouring across the river by now, and he knew that he might already be losing the element of surprise. He could have crossed an infantry force at the lower end of town at nine o'clock, and by eleven o'clock he could have supported it with artillery, but it would have been extremely vulnerable on that single lifeline and it might have taken several hours to clear the city of sharpshooters. Instead, just as pontoniers tied off the last of Franklin's bridges, Burnside decided to pound the offending houses to rubble, and he brought every gun that could bear on the water's edge into battery. For two hours nearly 150 cannon belched solid shot and shell into the buildings, the gunners taking careful aim now that the mists had cleared. Barksdale's men huddled wherever they could find solid cover while Union iron ate away walls, perforated rooftops, and shattered windows and doors. Some of the shells sparked fires, and the city choked beneath a pall of smoke and dust.

At about two o'clock the guns began falling silent. Confident engineers supposed those thousands of rounds had driven every Confederate from his nest or buried him in debris. The bridges boomed with

WHILE THE 50TH NEW YORK ENGINEERS STRUGGLED TO CONSTRUCT BRIDGES AT THE TOWN, MEMBERS OF THE 15TH NEW YORK ENGINEERS COMPLETED TWO BRIDGES A MILE BELOW TOWN. THEY ADDED A THIRD BRIDGE THE NEXT DAY.

(BL)

Unable to complete his bridges as long as Confederates held the town, Burnside shelled Fredericksburg with nearly 150 cannon. When the smoke cleared, Barksdale's men were still there.

(USAMHI)

sprinting feet once more, but as soon as the dull thud of hammers echoed across the flood a spattering of shots answered. Most of the sharpshooters remained in their dens, and all save a few Floridians—who refrained from firing lest they draw the artillery upon their heads again—started plugging away. The bridge builders would have no more of that and broke for cover.

Frustrated beyond belief, Burnside took a suggestion from his chief of artillery and ordered a brigade across the river in loose pontoon boats to storm the town. Under cover of yet another barrage, the 7th Michigan and 19th Massachusetts gathered on the bank to be ferried across by New York engineers. The frazzled artisans fled, but the Michigan colonel put a few dozen of his men in three or four pontoons anyway, and they poled themselves to the opposite bank. The colonel took the lead pontoon himself, but he was wounded in midstream, as were several others. The rest rushed gamely up the bank, though, and began kicking in doors. The remainder of the 7th Michigan and the 19th Massachusetts quickly followed, but they met stiff resistance and could not clear the town until they were reinforced by the 20th Massachusetts. At the middle bridge a hundred New Yorkers also poled their way over and began to roust the snipers from their nests on that end of town. Most of the Floridians and about sixty of the Mississippians eventually surrendered, while the rest of Barksdale's brigade pulled back to contest the Federals street by street.

14

# A WOMAN'S STORY

*Jane Beale, a resident of Fredericksburg, was at her home when the Union army first crossed the Rappahannock River on December 11th. She recounted that day's harrowing experiences in her diary.*

> *I scarcely knew where I was . . . the yard was filled with armed men, the trees were cut off at their tops and their branches lay around impeding our progress.*

We were aroused before day by Gen Lee's 'Signal guns,' but not knowing their special significance, we did not hurry ourselves-, until 'Martha' our chamber maid came in and said in a rather mournful tone, "Miss Jane the Yankees are coming, they have got two pontoons nearly across the river." before we were half dressed the heavy guns of the enemy began to pour their shot and shell upon our ill-fated town, and we hastily gathered our remaining garments, and rushed into our Basement for safety, on the first landing I remembered 'Julian' my sick boy and turned back to seek him. I met him with his youngest brother, half dressed with his clothes upon his arm, and tried to help him, but I was trembling so violently that I believe I was more indebted to him for assistance than he was to me. we sought the room often used for a kitchen, and as Susan made us a good fire (the fuel all being at hand), we drew around it, with our hearts earnestly seeking the protection of Heaven. our Pastor Mr. Lacy was still with us, and commenced in solemn but tender accents, repeating 'the 27th Psalm' as we all knew it we heartily responded to each verse. as the words "Tho an host should encamp against me, my heart shall not fear" were upon our lips, we startled from our seats by the crashing of glass and splintering of timber close beside us . . . . poor 'Lucy' lay on some straw put down on the damp floor, almost paralyzed with terror, while Helen G sought refuge close under the wall on the side from whence the shots seemed to come. Mr. Brent and Mr. Lacy came back and forth between us and the other room, trying occasionally to speak a word of comfort to us but too evidently depressed themselves, to inspire us with the smallest amount of home [sic: hope].

. . . brother John told us that the town was on fire in many places, a whole row of buildings on Main St were already burnt, and as my house had a shingled roof I thought we would soon be driven from it by fire also. Mr. Lacy left us with brother John and they could scarcely have got out of the town before the heavy Bombardment commenced again and the sound of 173 guns echoed in our ears, the shrieking of those shells, like a host of angry fiends rushing through the air, the crashing of the balls through the roof and upper stories of the house, I shall never forget to the day of my death, the agony and terror of the next four hours, is burnt in on my memory as with hot iron, I could not Pray, but only cry for mercy. About 6 o'clock the sound of my dear brother's voice was again heard at the door, and now there was no time for parley, "come he said instantly, I have got an Ambulance for you, the enemy is across the river and there is not a moment to lose," we struggled to our feet wrapped the blankets we had over our heads and crept out of the cellar door into our yard blinded by the light, after being so long confined to darkness, I scarcely knew where I was, indeed the strange sight that met my first bewildered gaze, might well have astonished me, the palings were all down the yard was filled with armed men, the trees were cut off at their tops and their branches lay around impeding our progress. the Ambulance was drawn up behind the School House and

## THE CITY TAKEN

General Woodbury had momentarily disappeared, but with the retreat of Barksdale's sharpshooters the New York engineers sprinted out again to complete the bridges. In the growing darkness the Union spearhead pushed the last Confederate defenders beyond the edge of the city. By nightfall four full Union brigades occupied Fredericksburg. Franklin crossed a brigade as well, but Burnside ordered the rest of the army to remain on the left bank of the river. He may have feared that darkness would render the deployment chaotic and invite an attack, or perhaps he wished to keep Lee wondering whether this might not be a mere diversion for a stronger attack somewhere else— somewhere like Skinker's Neck, where a Maine regiment had been corduroying roads all day to keep the Confederates off guard.

Had most of the army marched to the

we had to go through the whole length of the yard to get to it, some of the soldiers spoke to us and recommended haste as the enemy was coming up the hill not two squares off, our own men were evidently falling back, the town was to be given up to the enemy. We were shoved into the vehicle without much ceremony, and the horses dashed off at a speed that at another time would have alarmed me, but now seemed all too slow for our feverish impatience to be beyond the reach of those terrible shots which were still tearing through the streets of the town, one struck a building just as we passed it, another tore up the ground a short distance from us. I was greatly distressed to leave the servants but they said they were not afraid of the enemy and would go over the river if they were in greater danger here. As we passed beyond the line of the town and the turn of the road put the 'Willis Hill' Promontory of land, between us and the firing, a sense of security came into my mind and deep and heartfelt thankfulness for our deliverance from this great evil, carried my spirit to the throne of Heaven in humble grateful prayer. but new objects attracted my attention and claimed my sympathy here, crowds of women and children had sought refuge in this sheltered spot and as night drew on they were in great distress, they could not return to the town which was already in possession of the enemy, and they had fled too hastily to bring with them the comforts even the necessaries of life. Some few had stretched blue yarn counterpanes or pieces of old carpet over sticks, stuck in the ground—and the little ones were huddled together under these tents, the women were weeping the children crying loudly, I saw one walking along with a baby in her arms and another little one not three years old clinging to her dress and crying "I want to go home" My heart ached for them and if I could I would have stopped the Ambulance and taken them in, but I did not know then that I might not have to spend the night out in the open air myself . . . . we thought we would at least seek refuge in Mr. Temple's hospitable premises, and if the house was full he would let us stay in his barn, but when we drove up to the door the family rushed out and my dear friend Mrs. Temple carried me into the house almost in her arms, weeping as she went, at the idea of the dreadful peril to which we had been exposed all day. She gave up her most comfortable room for our accommodation and in a nice old-fashioned easy chair, before a blazing wood fire with my children around me, I ended the day so full of threatened danger and real horror in its beginning and its progress. I truly felt that praise for our deliverance was and ought to be the burthen of our song that night.

*The Diary of Jane Beale*

THE BATTLE FORCED FREDERICKSBURG RESIDENTS TO FLEE THEIR HOMES AND SEEK SHELTER IN OUTLYING AREAS.

(USAMHI)

right bank that night, Burnside might have been able to launch an attack early the next morning that would have caught Lee with as few as eighteen regiments protecting his right flank at Hamilton's Crossing, instead of the eighteen brigades poised there when he finally did attack. Stonewall Jackson's corps lay scattered from Guiney Station to Port Royal just then, while only one division of Longstreet's corps stood at Hamilton's Crossing, but before dawn on December 12 Lee sent for Jackson's two nearest divisions to strengthen that position.

The greater part of the Army of the Potomac finally thundered over the bridges the morning of the 12th, with Sumner's troops bivouacking in the city streets while Franklin's divisions spread out on the plain. Burnside seems to have recognized that the previous day's delay (including his failure to cross the army during the night) had probably destroyed any chance of catching Lee's army divided, so he started

AT THE SUGGESTION OF HIS CHIEF OF ARTILLERY, HENRY HUNT, BURNSIDE DETERMINED TO SEND INFANTRY ACROSS THE RIVER IN BOATS TO DISLODGE BARKSDALE'S MEN. COLONEL NORMAN HALL'S BRIGADE DREW THE DANGEROUS ASSIGNMENT.

(NPS)

the morning by formulating some subtle revisions in his battlefield choreography, conferring with officers who had seen the ground before. Now, instead of moving Sumner and Franklin directly against their respective goals, he proposed giving Franklin the principal role, allowing him to lead off with the largest part of the army. Franklin would sweep around Hamilton's Crossing and secure a new military road the Confederates had cut to connect the two wings of their army, threatening Lee's rear more by maneuver than by actual assault. As soon as Franklin had made a good start, Sumner would hit the heights on Lee's left, near the Marye mansion. It was the pugilistic equivalent of a left hook followed by a right cross—a favorite tactic of Burnside's.

While Burnside planned, his troops

BARKSDALE BATTLED THE UNION TROOPS IN TOWN UNTIL DARK, THEN WITHDREW TO MARYE'S HEIGHTS. HIS STUBBORN DEFENSE OF THE RIVER DELAYED BURNSIDE'S CROSSING BY A FULL DAY, GIVING LEE TIME TO COMPLETE HIS DEFENSIVE ARRANGEMENTS.

(HARPERS WEEKLY)

roamed the city, inspecting the damage. The riddled buildings sat almost entirely abandoned, and curious soldiers wandered through them, picking up a candlestick or a few pieces of silverware here and there, but the quest for souvenirs quickly escalated to plundering and wanton destruction. Virtually every home or business saw blue-clad looters who stuffed their haversacks with anything edible and their knapsacks with whatever might be worth a dollar. Furniture went flying into the streets, and whole libraries were overturned alongside it. Soldiers cavorted in civilian clothing, including dresses pulled over their uniforms, and one scavenger piled blankets and carpeting on the back of a stray horse, hoping apparently to sleep snugly for at least one night. A New Hampshire boy who would strangle from fever beneath a

WITH FREDERICKSBURG BURNING IN THE BACKGROUND, RUSH HAWKINS'S UNION BRIGADE CROSSED THE MIDDLE BRIDGE INTO TOWN ON THE NIGHT OF DECEMBER 11. MOST OF THE ARMY WOULD NOT CROSS UNTIL THE NEXT DAY.

(LC)

AFTER CROSSING THE RIVER, THE UNION ARMY PROCEEDED TO SACK THE TOWN. THEY SMASHED MIRRORS, BROKE FURNITURE, AND HAULED PIANOS INTO THE STREET. "THE SOLDIERS SEEMED TO DELIGHT IN DESTROYING EVERYTHING," WROTE ONE WITNESS.

(LC)

Mississippi live oak seven months hence cut a painting from its frame and tucked it into his knapsack, admitting to his very respectable parents that he would have stolen a lot more if he thought he could have smuggled it across the river. Burnside's provost marshal finally arrived and began lashing at looters with his riding crop; his guard details collected platoons of prisoners, and the marshal himself caught some mounted officers with plunder hanging from their saddles.

## THE FINAL PLAN OF ATTACK

Vandals were still rifling Fredericksburg closets that afternoon when Burnside rode down to Franklin's bridges. The racing winter sun neared the horizon already, and the general saw that there could be no attack that day, either, so he met with Franklin and his corps commanders to explain the differences in the latest orders for the assault. Two divisions of the Third Corps would move from Hooker's Center Grand Division to guard the bridgehead, allowing Franklin all six of his own big divisions to race around Hamilton's Crossing. When he was satisfied that his wishes were understood, Burnside rode back to speak with his other wing commanders.

Even as Burnside and Franklin scanned the wooded ridge that shielded the Confederate army, Southern horsemen flew downriver with instructions for Jackson's last two divisions to start for Hamilton's Crossing from Port Royal and Skinker's Neck. In a note to D. H. Hill, the commander of his most distant division (and his own brother-in-law), Stonewall revealed that their right flank seemed to be the target now; thanks partly to the houses that screened Sumner's divisions, the top Southern commanders suspected the movement on the city might have been no more than a feint.

The ridge on which Lee had perched his army was long and low, though it was tall enough by Tidewater standards and

LEE POSTED HIS TROOPS ON A SERIES OF HILLS SOUTH AND WEST OF TOWN. THIS VIEW, TAKEN FROM MARYE'S HEIGHTS, SHOWS THE DEADLY PLAIN UNION SOLDIERS WOULD HAVE TO CROSS TO ATTACK THE CONFEDERATE LINE.

(NA)

Thomas Cobb's Georgia brigade awaited the Federals in a sunken road bordered by a shoulder-high stone wall at the base of Marye's Heights. "I think my Brigade can whip ten thousand of them attacking us in front," Cobb wrote his wife prior to the battle. He was wrong: it whipped 40,000.

(USAMHI)

high enough even at its lowest point to offer a military advantage. It consisted of a series of connected hills. Those on the Confederate left, especially Marye's Heights, loomed quite steep, and here Longstreet arranged his defensive line in tiers. Infantry filled the Telegraph Road, a lane cut into the base of the hillside. The Telegraph Road turned parallel to the ridge here, its sunken bed protected by stone retaining walls. Riflemen squatted contentedly behind the downhill wall, the muzzles of their weapons gaping at the half mile of open, gently rising ground any Federal attack would have to cross.

Four more knobs rose from the ridge as it twisted its way to the southeast, each of them successively shorter than the one before. The Confederate right rested on Prospect Hill, a shallow plateau just behind Hamilton's Crossing. There stood Captain Hamilton's house and a cluster of Southern artillery that may have posed the greatest impediment to any passage around that flank. By nightfall of December 12 Ambrose Powell Hill covered the crossing with his six brigades. Another of Jackson's divisions backed him up, while those under Jubal Early and D. H. Hill had camped for the night only a few hours away.

Unless they marched completely around Lee's right, the Federals would face broad plains wherever they struck, yet Lee had said the terrain here worked against him. He had failed to convince Jefferson Davis to let him fall back to the North

Anna, where he would not have to worry so much about the enemy slipping behind him, so here he would make his stand.

## THE ORDERS

At his headquarters in the Phillips house, on high ground about a mile from the river, Burnside rose early on the morning of December 13 to dictate orders for his grand division commanders. He chose James A. Hardie, a staff brigadier and a West Point classmate of Franklin's, to carry the instructions for the left wing commander. Burnside asked Hardie to remain with Franklin during the day and telegraph news of his progress frequently. Hardie took the orders at 6:00 A.M., guiding his horse over a glaze of ice and mud.

Franklin's orders directed him to position his entire command "for a rapid movement down the old Richmond road," adding that he should "send out at once a division at least to pass below Smithfield and seize, if possible, the height near Captain Hamilton's, on this side of the Massaponax, taking care to keep it well supported and its line of retreat open." At the tail of the order Burnside alluded to holding Franklin's main body "in readiness to move at once, as soon as the fog lifts."

The written orders therefore suggested that Franklin's assault on Prospect Hill should commence immediately, in the fog, while the balance of the Left Grand Division should wait until visibility improved. Apparently Burnside intended to capture that dangerous concentration of cannon under cover of the fog, surprising the gunners before they could do much damage; by then the mists would probably have begun to dissipate, and Franklin could see where he was going with the rest of his wing. So, too, would Lee be able to witness Franklin's flank movement, which might convince him to shift troops from Marye's Heights.

Burnside and Franklin had discussed the battle plan the previous evening, and perhaps Burnside depended too heavily on Franklin's apparent comprehension of his wishes. But Franklin later claimed that, when Hardie arrived with the formal orders, sometime after seven o'clock, they contradicted his understanding of the plan: Franklin insisted he had been slated to launch an all-out assault on Lee's right, while the orders seemed to reduce his role to a diversion. For all his future complaints about the clarity of his orders, however, he asked no questions about them that morning, and within half an hour of Hardie's arrival Franklin had chosen George G. Meade's division of Pennsylvanians to lead the assault.

On the right, Burnside sent Sumner orders to attack Marye's Heights by way of the Telegraph and Orange Plank roads. With his penchant for understatement Burnside also told Sumner to begin his assault with "a division or more," though the artillery arrayed on the heights obviously called for more, but Burnside asked Sumner to hold off on the movement until he joined him at his headquarters.

BURNSIDE DIRECTED THE BATTLE FROM THE PHILLIPS HOUSE, EAST OF THE RIVER. TWO MONTHS LATER, UNION SOLDIERS ACCIDENTALLY SET FIRE TO THE HOUSE WHILE COOKING, DESTROYING IT.

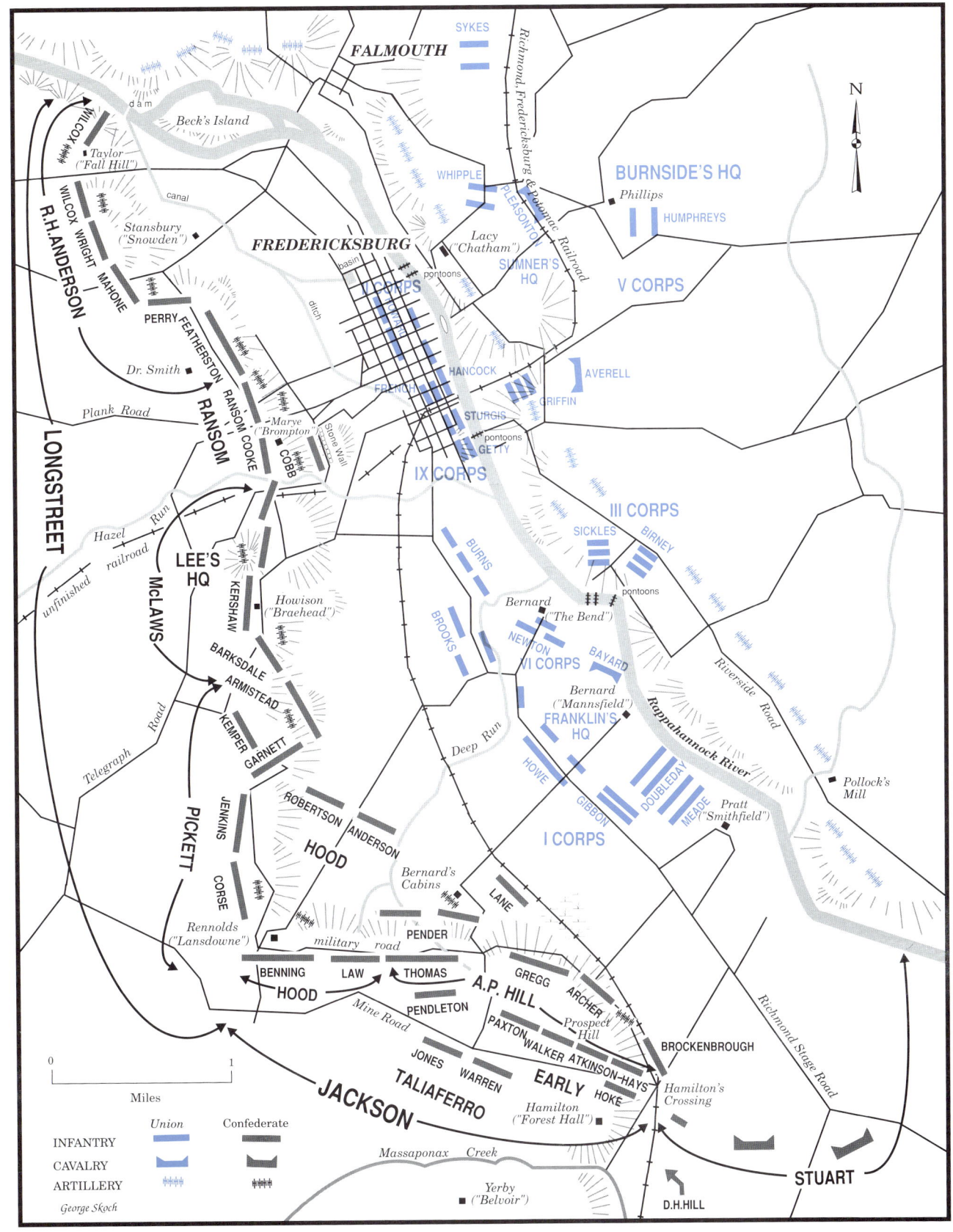

## ON THE EVE OF THE BATTLE: DAWN, DECEMBER 13

*Burnside is ready to attack. Franklin's grand division is massed around the Bernard mansion, "Mannsfield," two miles below Fredericksburg, while the troops of Sumner's grand division form ranks in the streets of the town. Hooker's troops remain on the east side of the river, ready to go where needed. Lee, meanwhile, has contracted his line, drawing Longstreet's corps to the left of Deep Run to make room for Jackson's corps, which arrives on December 12-13, and takes position on the right. Two brigades of Stuart's cavalry guard the Confederate right, near Massaponax Creek.*

WILLIAM B. FRANKLIN
(BL)

CONFEDERATE TROOPS AT HAMILTON'S CROSSING
(BL)

Franklin proved woefully unfamiliar with the lay of the land in front of him. The Richmond Stage Road followed the river for a couple of miles beyond Franklin's headquarters and a mile past the plantation known as Smithfield, whereupon it veered south, around Hamilton's Crossing. Two other roads branched off in that direction before that point, however, and these appear to have confused both Franklin and Burnside. In an earlier order Burnside had described Franklin's route as "down the Richmond road, in the direction of the railroad," but the stage road ran parallel to the railroad all along the front here, even after the turn at Hamilton's Crossing. Evidently Burnside mistook the Mine Road—the second of those right turns—for the stage road, for that road did cross the railroad at Hamilton's. (On his map of the battle a division commander on Franklin's front labeled that the Bowling Green Road, which was another name for the Richmond Stage Road.) An assault by Franklin's command on both sides of this road might have been quite effective, but Franklin erred even further, choosing the first road to the right. This was little more than a local farm lane that turned from the stage road abreast of Smithfield—rather than below Smithfield, as Burnside had instructed. Nor did this lane flank the position at Hamilton's Crossing; instead, it ran head-on into Stonewall Jackson's infantry.

It was nine o'clock before Meade deployed his division. He commanded fifteen regiments, most of them veteran Pennsylvania Reserves who had fought from the outset of the war, and that morning the three brigades brought about 6,500 rifles to bear. After reaching the erroneous turn Franklin had indicated, Meade called for pioneers to chop passageways through the thick hedges that bordered the highway, and he asked for engineers to fill the deep ditches, so artillery might follow him. All of that done, he arranged two of his brigades in columns of attack three hundred yards apart and turned the third perpendicular to these two, facing his vulnerable left flank. Even as he moved out, the last stragglers of D. H. Hill's division dropped, breathless, alongside their comrades behind Hamilton's Crossing. Had Franklin followed the route Burnside intended, he would have run right into these exhausted troops. Jackson's corps was now completely reunited, and his 39,000 men lay four and five brigades deep along the final mile and a half of that forested ridge. J. E. B. Stuart extended the Confederate right toward the Massaponax with two brigades of cavalry.

Meade had no more than begun his advance when shells started dropping into the ranks from his left and rear. Under John Pelham, the 24-year-old major commanding

Stuart's horse artillery, two Confederate guns had ranged ahead from Stuart's line to pester the Federal assault. Pelham's shells raked Meade's first two brigades, leaving the Pennsylvanian no choice but to deal with the irksome brace before continuing. Skirmishers trotted out from Meade's perpendicular brigade and Union artillery turned against Pelham's pair of cannon, but the young major kept his guns moving between rounds, preventing the Yankees from finding his range. His sporadic fire nonetheless kept Meade motionless for more than an hour, and Pelham still blazed away with one gun after the other was disabled, but finally Stuart ordered him to bring the surviving piece back to safety. With Jackson's defensive line complete, there seemed no point in delaying the enemy further.

GEORGE G. MEADE

(BL)

Meade's corps commander, John F. Reynolds, offered him what support he could by throwing Abner Doubleday's division just below Smithfield to bar any assault along the stage road and by posting John Gibbon's division to Meade's right and rear. Meade would bear the brunt of the effort, though, and once the adjoining units had reached their positions he started forward.

When they stepped off again, Meade's men encountered a soggy lowland just before the railroad. The marshy ground broadened out beyond the tracks, where accumulated runoff from the ridge offered uncomfortable passage in the December cold. Not wishing to subject his own men to a position in the bog, and doubting the enemy could traverse it, A. P. Hill had allowed a six-hundred-yard gap between the front-line brigades of James H. Lane and James J. Archer. As luck would have it, that is precisely where Meade's attack struck, and the Pennsylvanians waded deep into Confederate lines before they met much resistance. The third brigade swung behind Archer's, gobbling up scores of Georgians and Tennesseeans and driving three of Archer's regiments out of their rude breastworks. Meade's leading brigade wheeled to the right, causing even greater trouble among Lane's North Carolinians, while the other Keystone brigade rolled straight ahead into the void. It was begin-

THOMAS J. "STONEWALL" JACKSON

(THE VALENTINE MUSEUM)

# DEATH HAS BEEN DOING FEARFUL WORK TODAY

*Among the Union soldiers attacking Stonewall Jackson's line was a young Pennsylvanian named Jacob Heffelfinger. In the following diary passage, written while the battle still raged, Heffelfinger describes the Union army's initial success at Prospect Hill and its ultimate repulse.*

4 1/2 P.M.—The battle has raged fiercely today. The rebels occupy an advantageous position. Our troops are on an open plain, while they occupy a ridge in our front, and are sheltered by dense wood but about 1 1/2 P.M. one part of the line made a forward movement, our division, as usual, taking the advance. This was a fearful movement. We left the field over which we advanced, thickly strewn with our dead and wounded. We drove the rebels from their position in the rail-road cut at the edge of the wood. On entering the woods our line was thrown into confusion by a misunderstanding of orders, but our men pushed on boldly and reached the summit of the hill. During the confusion I received a shot through both legs, completely disabling me. Our men were soon after attacked by the enemy in heavy force, and being weakened by the great slaughter in our ranks while advancing, and wholly without support they were driven back over me in disorder. All that we gained at so fearful a cost is lost. I am still lying where I fell. The rebels have advanced a line over me, so that I am a prisoner. I am now exposed to the fire of our artillery which is fearfully destructive. Death has been doing fearful work today.

*Jacob Heffelfinger,
7th Pennsylvania Reserve*

JACOB HEFFELFINGER

(B. N. MILLER)

# A LETTER FROM THE BATTLEFIELD

*A soldier in the Pee Dee Artillery of South Carolina wrote his father the night of the battle, describing his experiences in repelling the Union attack at Prospect Hill.*

CAMP NEAR FREDERICKSBURG, DECEMBER 13, 1862 - SATURDAY NIGHT

DEAR FATHER -
I promised to write you immediately after the fight. All day yesterday we lay in position. Today I have been in the hottest fight I have ever heard of. From ten o'clock this morning till an hour or two since shot and shell, and Minie balls, having been perfectly hailing around me. All the other fights crowded into one would hardly make anything to be compared to today's fight. Our battery has lost three men killed and sixteen wounded, eighteen or twenty horse, one limber and one caisson blown up, and one gun disabled . . . . A piece of

shell went through my coat sleeve; it stung a little. A Minie ball went through the ramrod, and it or a splinter struck me on the head. I was by the gun looking at the Yankees when a great piece of shell, big as my two fists, came along and knocked a spoke out of the wheel, and it or a piece of the spoke, or something else, hit me square in the breast. I did not know whether I was mortally wounded or not, but after a while I opened my shirt, and found that the skin was not bruised. I saw a piece of shell go a "kiting" by my leg, missing it an inch or two. That is only a few of the narrow escapes that I made today. The trees around our guns were literally torn to pieces and the ground plowed up. I have been several times covered with dirt, and had it knocked in my eyes and mouth . . . .

PROSPECT HILL AS IT APPEARS TODAY

(NPS)

We were posted on a chain of hills. Just in the edge of the woods before us was a wide level plain extending to the river, some three or five miles wide. I could see fully half the whole Yankee army, reserves and all. It was a grand sight seeing them come in position this morning; but it seemed that that host would eat us up any how. I felt uneasy until I saw Gen. Lee, and right behind him the "Old Stonewall," riding up and down our lines, looking at the foe as cooly and calmly as if they were only going to have a general muster. The Yankee batteries came into position beautifully, and commenced shelling the woods we were in. It was hard to take it, but we had strict orders not to fire. Their infantry advanced in beautiful order. When one thousand yards distant we poured a perfect storm of shell into them from fifty or one hundred guns, but on they came. Our infantry was too much for them they had to leave. Oh! it did me good to see the rascals run; but here comes a fresh line. Far as the eye can reach the line extends. They have the fate of their predecessors, but another new line advances. I had been uneasy, perhaps scared before, but now had death or defeat been offered me I would have taken the former. Some of our bravest were down . . . . Pegram's men (a Virginia battery stationed by our side on the right) had left their guns. Capt. Pegram wrapped his battle flag around him, walking up and down among his deserted guns. It was a time to test a man's courage. Our cannon flamed and roared, and the roar of musketry was terrific. The foe halts, wavers and flies. We double charging our gun, pour the canister among them. As they get out of range of that we send them an occasional shell to help them on. "Cease firing!" What means that yell to the right. No one answers, nor do we need an answer, for our gallant boys are seen pouring from the woods, double quicking on the charge. On they go, (Gregg's brigade leading) nearly up to the Yankee batteries. How my heart did beat then. My hat couldn't stay on my head. I would have hollered if I had been killed for it the next minute, simply because I couldn't help it.

Affectionately yours,
BEN

*Published in the Charleston Daily Courier, December 30, 1862*

UNION TROOPS CHARGE ACROSS THE R.F. & P. RAILROAD IN THEIR ATTACK ON STONEWALL JACKSON'S POSITION AT PROSPECT HILL.

(BL)

JOHN PELHAM
(THE VALENTINE MUSEUM)

ning to look to Meade as though his assault might succeed despite mistakes and delays, but the general could not see the three lines of Confederates that lay in the woods beyond.

Before long, however, Meade's onrushing riflemen discovered the first of those Confederates in the forest. Maxcy Gregg's five South Carolina regiments lay resting in the new military road Burnside sought, their arms stacked at Gregg's insistence to avoid an accidental volley into the backs of the front-line brigades. The collision surprised the Pennsylvanians almost as much as the recumbent South Carolinians, but the Yankees leveled a furious fire and scattered the first regiment while the rest of Gregg's men ran for their weapons. Gregg, who was forty-eight and rather deaf, thought they had fallen into the tragic error he had most feared: he anticipated that no enemy would burst out of the woods unless retreating Confederates preceded them, so he rode into his troops to stop the firing. Galloping about in full regalia, he drew a flurry of Union fire and fell from the saddle with a bullet in the spine while his fleeing men streamed past him.

That was Meade's high-water mark. The survivors of Gregg's brigade rallied, and two brigades from nearby divisions came to their assistance—including the one that had won Stonewall Jackson his nickname seventeen months before. That blunted the Pennsylvanians' momentum, and a Georgia brigade filed down to confront Meade's right-hand regiments. Artillery on Prospect Hill began to harry Meade's third brigade, on his left, while six regiments of Georgians and Virginians groped through the brush to contend with that side of the breach. Meade directed his brigadier on the left, Conrad F. Jackson, to work his way uphill until he could swing behind the troublesome guns and capture them, but General Jackson was killed just as he began the movement. His men advanced a little farther without him, coming to a halt when the Confederate reinforcements stalled the leading brigade.

The Pennsylvanians shot it out with nearly twice their number while thousands more Southerners stood ready to take them on if they came any farther. Yet Franklin never dispatched a man from Doubleday's

MAXCY GREGG
(BL)

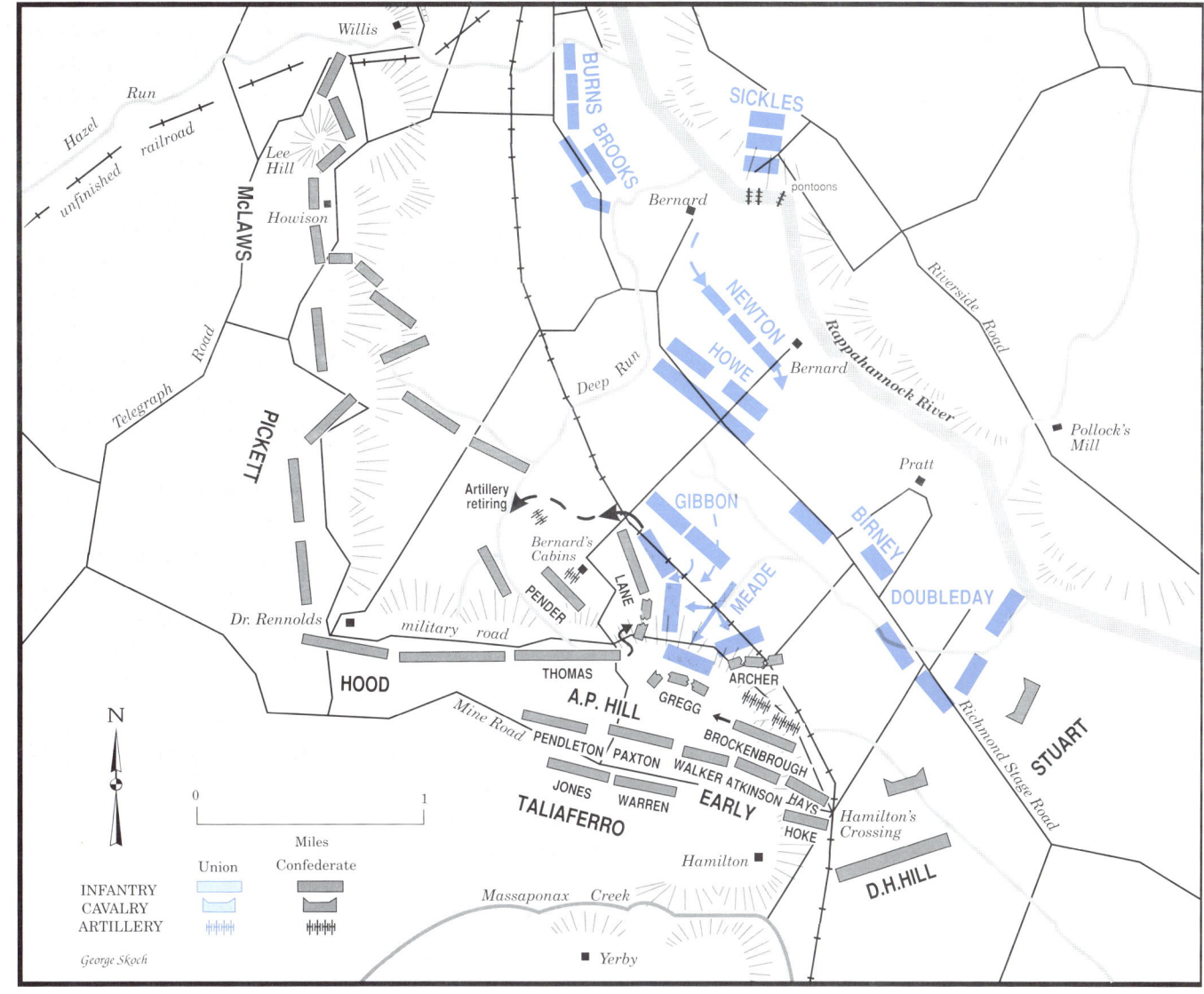

**MEADE BREACHES HILL'S LINE: DECEMBER 13, 1:00 P.M.**
After an hour-long artillery duel, Meade's division goes forward, penetrating a 600-yard gap in A.P. Hill's line. Lane's right flank is turned, while Gregg's and Archer's brigades are driven back. Gibbon advances to support Meade on the right, engaging a portion of Lane's brigade at the railroad, while Doubleday's division moves downriver to secure the intersection recently vacated by Pelham. Smith's Sixth Corps remains quietly in position near the bridgehead, while Birney's division of Hooker's grand division crosses the river and moves up in rear of Meade.

division to Meade's assistance, and Gibbon's division made no progress at all on Meade's right, where it faced the three regiments of Lane's brigade that Meade had not scattered and other Southern units on Lane's left. Gibbon wasted his strength in three piecemeal attacks on the railroad embankment, and one after the other his first two brigades fell apart. The third barely reached the tracks, but Gibbon could go no farther because no one had advanced to protect his right flank: the nearest friendly troops lounged half a mile behind him. All or part of five other Union divisions—upwards of 40,000 officers and men—lay within a mile of

John Robinson's brigade advances to cover Meade's retreat. As Robinson's horse falls to the ground, pinning its rider, Colonel Charles Collis snatches the flag of the 114th Pennsylvania Infantry and leads it forward against the advancing Confederate line.

(NPS)

*JACKSON COUNTER-ATTACKS: DECEMBER 13, 1:30 P.M.*
*Jackson counters Meade's attack by advancing Early's and Taliaferro's divisions. Disorganized, tired, and outnumbered, Meade's men fall back to the railroad and then to the Bernard house, where they reform. Atkinson's brigade pursues Meade onto the plain but quickly retires to the railroad when confronted by Birney's division and by Union artillery fire. After briefly securing a lodgement along the railroad, Gibbon too must fall back and reform near the Bernard house.*

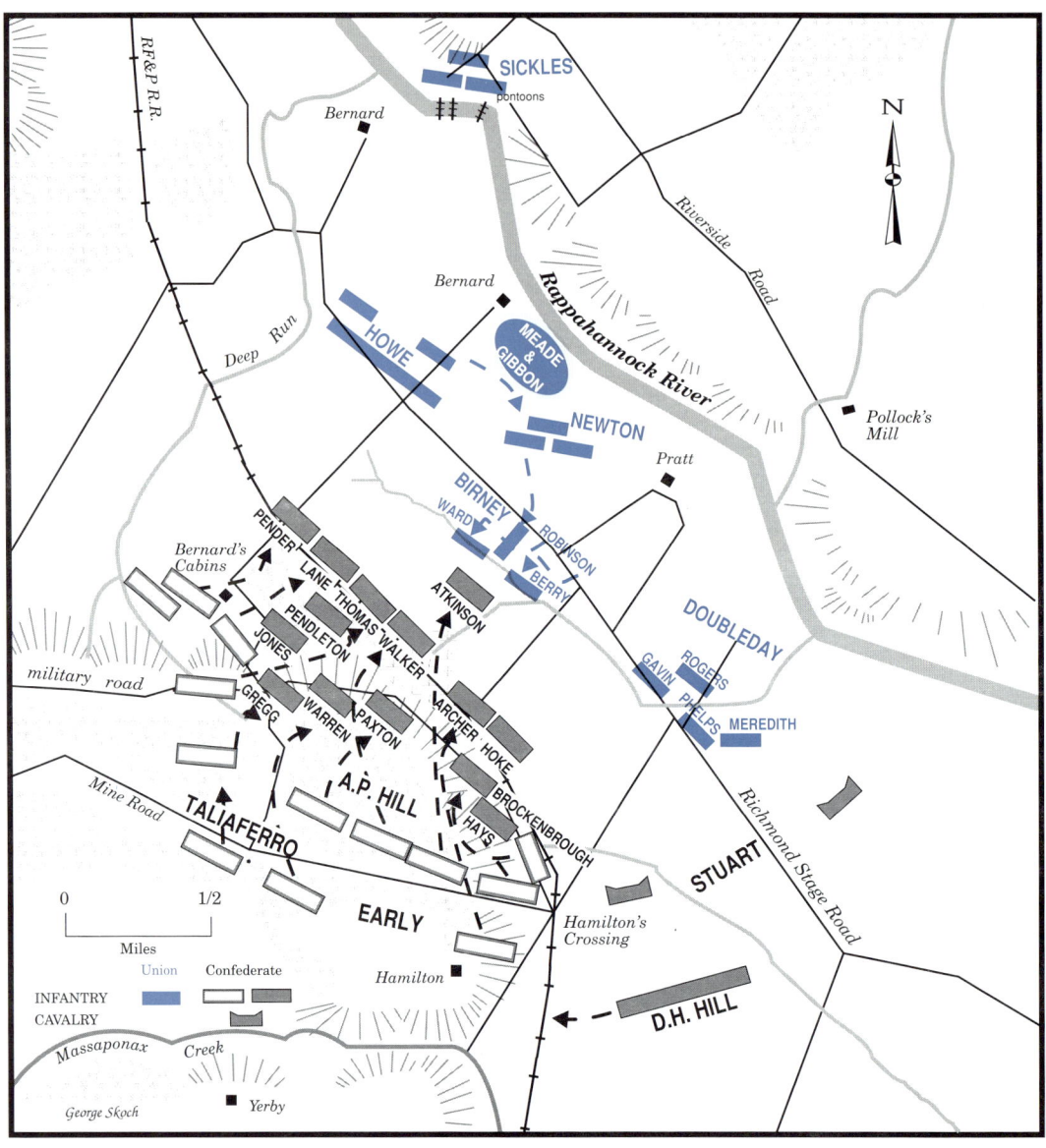

Meade's fight, but despite an appeal for help the only practical assistance Meade received came from fewer than two thousand men in Gibbon's surviving brigade.

Meade's men began to run out of ammunition. More than a quarter of his division lay dead or wounded now, while the Confederate ranks kept swelling, and finally the Pennsylvanians began backing out of their hard-fought forest. The retreat quickly degenerated into a rout, though, with men running pell-mell for the rear.

Gibbon's last brigade helped discourage Confederate pursuit for a time, but then it fled, too. One of David Birney's Third Corps brigades came up to cover the retreat, and a couple of Birney's regiments fanned out in an unsuccessful attempt to stay Meade's fugitives. Birney's men could only fill the void left by their frantic comrades, who did not stop until they had crossed the stage road. A Confederate counterattack dogged the shattered Federal line, taking up whole companies of Meade's lagging troops, but a point-blank blast from First Corps artillery and a steady fire from Birney's infantry stopped it.

It was now two o'clock. Like many of his senior officers, Meade felt he could have broken the Southern line with support from available troops, and he burst into General Reynolds's headquarters, raging over the failure to send him timely assistance. For three hours, though, William Franklin had been feeding James Hardie encouraging information to send to Burnside, including the news that the enemy was gathering for an attack on the Federals' extreme left. Supposing, perhaps, that Lee had begun swinging his strength to the southern end of his line, Burnside took that good news as his cue for launching Sumner's attack.

## THE STONE WALL: FRENCH'S ATTACK

Sumner's troops lay, cold and a little nervous, in the crowded lee of the city's houses, which hid all but their pickets from the Confederates. A hard frost the previous night had robbed them of much of their sleep, but they could neither warm themselves nor even boil coffee, lest the smoke from their fires reveal their numbers and draw fire. Many who had wandered away from their commands the night before had not returned. After sleeping with muddy feet in the beds of absent citizens, they resumed rummaging through the homes, pilfering whatever they fancied and vandalizing what they pleased. At the bridgeheads stood growing mountains of property confiscated from those brazen skulkers who tried to carry their plunder to the rear.

According to the morning's orders the commander of the Second Corps, General Couch, had formed William French's division along Fredericksburg's outermost streets. French's three brigades consisted of thirteen regiments from every state between Connecticut and the Wabash, including Delaware and West Virginia. Most of them had seen the Peninsula and Maryland campaigns, but the four biggest regiments consisted of nine-month militiamen from Pennsylvania and New Jersey.

Just beyond French's waiting lines the houses petered out and a broad plain opened, cut by a millrace that skirted the city's perimeter. Normally this waterway would have been full, but Federal engineers had partially closed the floodgate and drained the sluice somewhat. On the far side of the ditch the ground rose sharply, offering protection from enemy fire, and a quarter mile beyond that sat Marye's

IN ORDER TO REACH MARYE'S HEIGHTS, UNION SOLDIERS HAD TO CROSS AN OPEN PLAIN NEARLY ONE-HALF MILE IN LENGTH. NOT ONE REACHED THE STONE WALL.

(NA)

Heights and the sunken Telegraph Road. In that road crouched Thomas R. R. Cobb's Georgia brigade and the 24th North Carolina, their ranks hidden by the retaining wall. Another rank of Confederate infantry supported artillery that topped the crest, as well. William Street ran from the heart of the city toward the Sunken Road, passing beyond it to become the Orange Plank Road; Hanover Street paralleled it a couple of blocks to the south. The bridges on those streets and one other provided the only means of crossing the icy millrace, so when French received his final orders for the assault he filed his brigades across them.

James Longstreet had spent nearly three weeks perfecting his defenses on Marye's Heights. Just before the battle he had spoken to his artillery chief about using an overlooked cannon, suggesting that he place it to bear on the broad plain behind the city. Years later Longstreet remembered that his artilleryman assured him that the plain was already closely covered, promising that "a chicken could not live on that field when we open on it."

JAMES LONGSTREET
(USAMHI)

Shortly before noon Longstreet directed his gunners to begin dropping shells into the streets where he could see Union soldiers, hoping to create a diversion for Jackson's benefit. The moment he chose to open fire happened to be the same instant that French's skirmishers began jogging out of the city, with the dense, dark brigades following. Longstreet felt the sensation of having upset a beehive.

The skirmishers trotted across the ditch on one good bridge, but the boards of the other had been taken up and hundreds of men had to tiptoe across on the stringers. Meanwhile, shells from batteries on the heights began bursting in the ranks.

Once across the ditch, French formed his first brigade under the protection of the long bluff, and when he gave the word nearly two thousand men surged grimly forward with rifles on their shoulders and bayonets fixed. A hail of shell burst immediately from the heights, blowing great gaps in the ranks, but the Federals pounded onward without pausing to fire a shot, hoping to close with the enemy quickly. Muddy ground sucked at wet brogans with every step the Yankees took. Their entire route lay uphill, with the grade worsening steadily. Heavy overcoats, equipment, and ammunition bore down on those winded Northerners, and occasionally they had to stop to tear down fences. All the while iron burst and flew about them, changing from shell to canister that swept their lines like gigantic shotgun blasts. The gasping, sweating survivors reached a second shelf of land a hundred yards from the Sunken Road, and here they lingered another moment.

Burnside supposed that the greatest impediments to his advance were those he could detect with his binoculars: the artillery on the heights and the unprotected second line of infantry. Although Burnside and many of his subordinates had sojourned in Falmouth and Fredericksburg the previous summer, no one seems to have counted on the millrace or the hundreds of riflemen hidden in the Sunken Road. As soon as French's leading brigadier waved his men over that last swale they were met by a blinding flash and a deafening din, as though they had been struck by a lightning bolt. Pale blue overcoats reeled, fell, and tumbled, and the whole line staggered, wavering like a ribbon in the wind. More crashing volleys drove them back to the swale, and that was as far as they

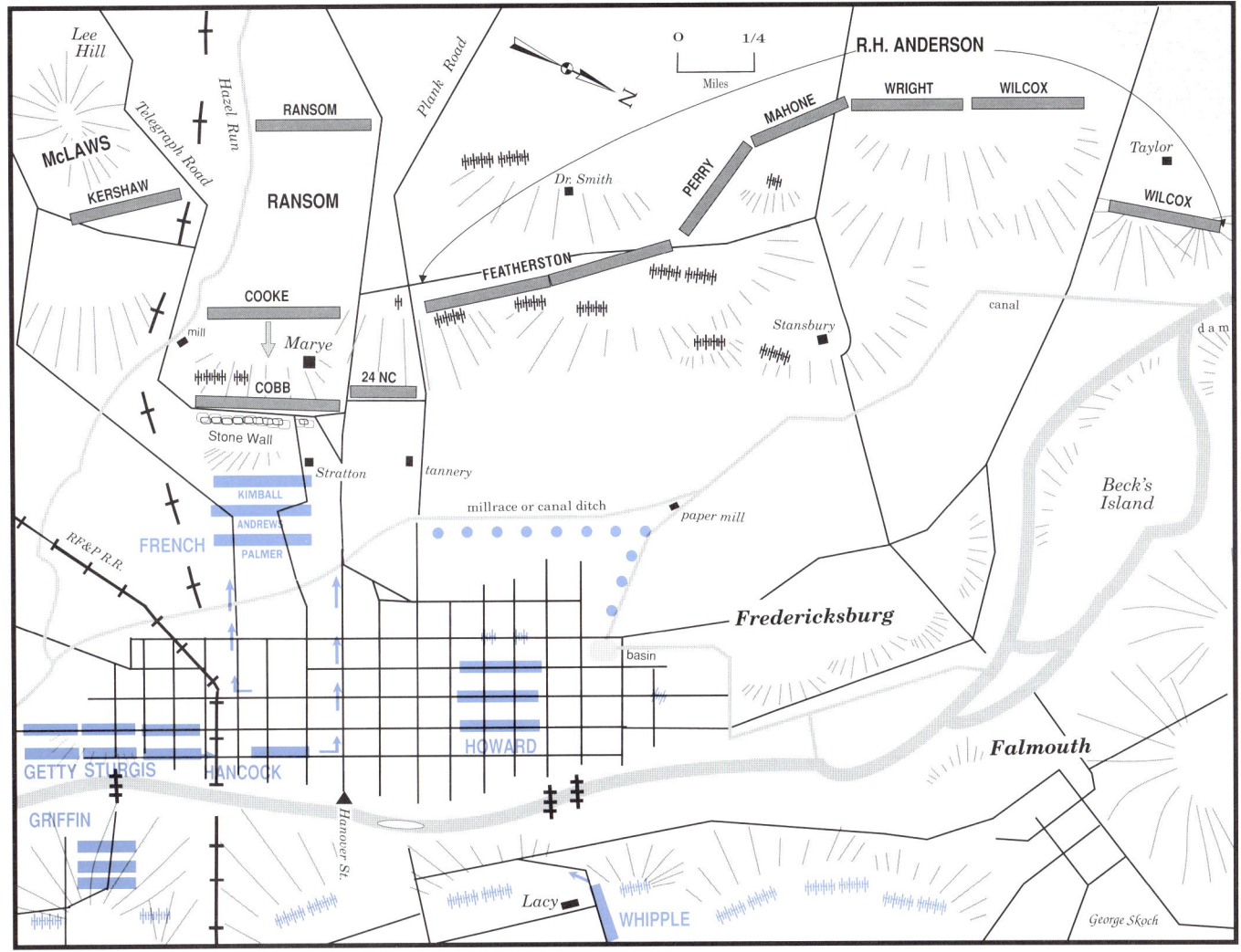

**FRENCH ATTACKS MARYE'S HEIGHTS: DECEMBER 13, NOON – 1 P.M.**
At noon French leaves the town, forms his division in the shelter of the millrace, and advances to attack Marye's Heights. Kimball's brigade leads the attack, followed by Andrews and Palmer. They are stopped short of their objective by Cobb's infantry brigade in the Sunken Road and by the Washington Artillery on the heights. As the attacks develop, Cooke's brigade moves up to the crest of the ridge to support Cobb's men in the road below.

would go. The brigadier, Nathan Kimball, quickly calculated that a quarter of his troops had already fallen; the survivors threw themselves down and started firing futilely into the cloud of smoke before them.

General Kimball glanced behind him in time to see the next brigade rise over the bluff and trot forward, heads bowed before the gale of canister. The script called for this next brigade, under Colonel James Andrews, to hang 150 yards behind Kimball, and when Andrews reached that distance he called a halt. He had but three regiments left (his own, the 1st Delaware, had gone in with the skirmishers), and as these Yankees stood to fire over their comrades' heads the Confederates rained iron and lead on their exposed position. Before long Colonel Andrews moved his men up

# THE ATTACK ON MARYE'S HEIGHTS: A CONFEDERATE PERSPECTIVE

*A*t dawn the next morning, December 13th, in the fresh and nipping air, I stepped upon the gallery overlooking the heights back of the little old-fashioned town of Fredericksburg. Heavy fog and mist hid the whole plain between the heights and the Rappahannock, but under cover of that fog and within easy cannon-shot lay Burnside's army. Along the heights, to the right and left of where I was standing, extending a length of nearly five miles, lay Lee's army.

The bugles and the drum corps of the respective armies were now sounding reveille, and the troops were preparing for their early meal. All knew we should have a battle today and a great one, for the enemy had crossed the river in immense force, upon his pontoons during the night. On the Confederate side all was ready, and the shock was awaited with stubborn resolution. Last night we had spread our blankets upon the bare floor in the parlor of Marye's house, and now our breakfast was being prepared in its fireplace, and we were impatient to have it over. After hastily dispatching this light meal of bacon and corn-bread, the colonel, chief bugler, and I (the adjutant of the battalion) mounted our horses and rode out to inspect our lines . . . .

At 12 o'clock the fog had cleared, and while we were sitting in Marye's yard smoking our pipes, after a lunch of hard crackers, a courier came to Colonel Walton, bearing a dispatch from General Longstreet for General Cobb, but, for our information as well, to be read and then given to him. It was as follows: "Should General Anderson, on your left, be compelled to fall back to the second line of heights, you must conform to his movements." Descending the hill into the sunken road, I made my way through the troops, to a little house where General Cobb had his headquarters, and handed him the dispatch. He read it carefully, and said, "Well! if they wait for me to fall back, they will wait a long time."

Hardly had he spoken, when a brisk skirmish fire was heard in front, toward the town, and looking over the stone wall we saw our skirmishers falling back, firing as they came; at the same time the head of a Federal column was seen emerging from one of the streets of the town. They came on at the double-quick, with loud cries of "Hi! Hi! Hi!" which we could distinctly hear. Their arms were carried at "right shoulder shift," and their colors were aslant the

CONFEDERATE ARTILLERY IN ACTION ON MARYE'S HEIGHTS.
(BL)

shoulders of the color-sergeants. They crossed the canal at the bridge, and getting behind the bank to the low ground to deploy, were almost concealed from our sight. It was 12:30 p.m., and it was evident that we were now going to have it hot and heavy.

The enemy, having deployed, now showed himself above the crest of the ridge and advanced in columns of brigades, and at once our guns began their deadly work with shell and solid shot. How beautifully they came on! Their bright bayonets glistening in the sunlight made the line look like a huge serpent of blue and steel. The very force of their onset leveled the broad fences bounding the small fields and gardens that interspersed the plain. We could see our shells bursting in their ranks, making great gaps; but on they came, as though they would go straight through and over us. Now we gave them canister, and that staggered them. A few more paces onward and the Georgians in the road below us rose up, and, glancing an instant along their rifle barrels, let loose a storm of lead into the faces of the advance brigade. This was too much; the column hesitated, and then, turning, took refuge behind the bank.

But another line appeared from behind the crest and advanced gallantly, and again we opened our guns upon them, and through the smoke we could discern the red breeches of the "Zouaves," and hammered away at them especially. But this advance, like the preceding one, although passing the point reached by the first column, and doing and daring all that brave men could do, recoiled under our canister and the bullets of the infantry in the road, and fell back in great confusion. Spotting the fields in our front, we could detect little patches of blue—the dead and wounded of the Federal infantry who had fallen facing the very muzzles of our guns.

Cooke's brigade of Ransom's division was now placed in the sunken road with Cobb's men. At 2 p.m. other columns of the enemy left the crest and advanced to the attack; it appeared to us that there was no end of them. On they came in beautiful array and seemingly more determined to hold the plain than before; but our fire was murderous, and no troops on earth could stand the *feu d'enfer* we were giving them. In the foremost line we distinguished the green flag with the golden harp of old Ireland, and we knew it to be Meagher's Irish brigade. The gunners of the two rifle pieces . . . were directed to turn their guns against this column; but the gallant enemy pushed on beyond all former charges, and fought and left their dead within five and twenty paces of the sunken road . . . .

The sharp-shooters having got range of our embrasures, we began to suffer. Corporal Ruggles fell mortally wounded, and Perry, who seized the rammer as it fell from Ruggles's hand, received a bullet in the arm. Rodd was holding "vent," and away went his "crazy bone." In quick succession Everett, Rossiter, and Kursheedt were wounded. Falconer in passing in rear of the guns was struck behind the ear and fell dead. We were now so short-handed that every one was in the work, officers and men putting their shoulders to the wheels and running up the guns after each recoil. The frozen ground had given way and was all slush and mud. We were compelled to call upon the infantry to help us at the guns. Eshleman crossed over from the right to report his guns nearly out of ammunition; the other officers reported the same. They were reduced to a few solid shot only. It was now 5 o'clock, p.m., and there was a lull in the storm. The enemy did not seem inclined to renew his efforts, so our guns were withdrawn one by one, and the batteries of Woolfolk and Moody were substituted . . . .

After withdrawing from the hill the command was placed in bivouac, and the men threw themselves upon the ground to take a much-needed rest. We had been under the hottest fire men ever experienced for four hours and a half, and our loss had been three killed and twenty-four wounded . . . . One gun was slightly disabled, and we had exhausted all of our canister, shell and case shot, and nearly every solid shot in our chests. At 5:30 another attack was made by the enemy, but it was easily repulsed, and the battle of Fredericksburg was over, and Burnside was baffled and defeated.

*William Miller Owen,
"A Hot Day on Marye's Heights"*

*How beautifully they came on! Their bright bayonets glistening in the sunlight made the line look like a huge serpent of blue and steel.*

THE MARYE HOUSE ("BROMPTON")

(USAMHI)

# THE ATTACK ON MARYE'S HEIGHTS: A UNION PERSPECTIVE

*"Cheer up, my hearties! cheer up! This is something we must all get used to. Remember, this brigade has never been whipped, and don't let it be whipped today."*

Next morning, December 13th, the city was enveloped in a heavy fog, which did not lift, if my recollection is clear, until ten o'clock or later. As far as we could see in either direction stood a continuous line of soldiers in readiness to start to the field of action. Mounted officers and orderlies were continually passing back and forth along the lines, while some of the regimental officers and privates, tired of standing in the ranks, dropped out and sought a seat upon the curb or a near-by door step. Among those who had taken a resting place was a surgeon, upon whose face I noticed was depicted an intense feeling of sadness. Perhaps he could not help it, for we all knew that some of us would soon be badly wounded if not instantly killed. Yet this solemn fact did not make all men gloomy. The most lively fellows mimicked the whizzing noise of an occasional round shot or shell in its arched flight high over the housetops, or cracked jokes with their comrades . . . .

Presently is heard the command, "Attention!". Every lounger springs to his place. We are ordered to prime. Every musket is raised and every man caps his piece. Our Colonel made some remarks, telling us to shoot low and try to wound a man in preference to killing him. Noticing a red colored scarf about my neck, he ordered me to take it off, saying it would make a good target for the enemy. The scarf disappeared. Suspense is intense. Finally, the long-expected, much-dreaded command, "Forward!" is passed from officer to officer standing at the head of their Companies. With an ominous silence akin to a funeral procession, General Kimball began the perilous march down Caroline street . . . . Reaching what I will call Railroad avenue, the column filed to the right and out that thoroughfare to begin the attack. I think I am telling the plain truth when I say that during that short march many of those men silently offered up to the Almighty their last prayer on earth. Our regiment was about to receive its first baptism of fire, and every one knew it.

. . . Shells and solid shot from the enemy's heavy guns now came crashing through brick walls and pounded in the street around about us. The first wounded man I saw was hurrying down the sidewalk with one hand pressed against a wound in his breast, inquiring for a hospital.

At the edge of the town we passed General Kimball facing us, in his saddle, who addressed his men in these words, which I never forgot:

"Cheer up, my hearties! cheer up! This is something we must all get used to. Remember, this brigade has never been whipped, and don't let it be whipped today."

No wild hurrah went up in response. Every face wore an expression of seriousness and dread . . . .

. . . A few steps further and we are out of the town, in the open fields, in full view of the enemy. While the brigade is coming into position, at double-quick, to assault the Confederate fortifications around Marye's Heights, the artillerymen on the summit are turning their guns upon us, and with effect. To facilitate our progress in the charge, haversacks and blankets are now thrown away. The company commanders shout sharply to their men to keep the regiments in line as they advance to the attack. Screeching like demons in the air, solid shot, shrapnel and shells from the batteries on the hills strike the ground in front of us, behind us, and cut gaps in the ranks. See there! A field officer has been struck by one of the missiles and a couple of men who have raised him to his feet are calling loudly for more help to get him off the field. As the line advances up the slope, men wounded and dead drop from the ranks.

It is not every man that can face danger like this. I saw a few so overcome by fear that they fell prostrate upon the ground as if dead. I have seen men drop upon their knees and pray loudly for deliverance, when courage and bravery, not supplication, was the duty of the moment.

Hark! There's one of my comrades, Johnny Brayerton, praying, too, perhaps for the first time in his life. It was a short one:

"Oh, Lord, dear, good Lord!" he cried.

But Johnny at that trying moment was as brave as he was devout, and kept his place in the front rank. Not a gun was fired . . . until the brigade reached the crest of the hill, when, like a burst of thunder, the roar of musketry became almost deafening. It seemed to me every soldier, after firing his piece, had thrown himself flat upon the ground to avoid the enemy's bullets, and I did not see how I could possibly load and fire by lying down in that crouching column of men. To stand up boldly along that firing line—the dead line—was almost certain death, so I ran to a blacksmith shop some distance to my right, where, with a number of other soldiers who had taken refuge there, we banged away at the rebels; but they were so securely and safely entrenched behind a great stone wall, that I believe every man in the firing line felt that there was not hope of a victory . . . .

The little frame building from which we were firing was by no means bullet-proof, yet we felt much safer there than standing out in full view of the enemy. Down goes one of our party, shot through the head.

I know not for what reason, but I stopped firing a few moments, and stood over the lifeless form of the unknown soldier with a sort of fascination, wondering who he could be; wondering what mother's boy had been added to the roll of the dead . . . .

"There they come!" someone shouted, and looking back toward the city, we saw another long line of reinforcements charging up the slope. Lustily they were cheered as they advanced, and I noticed a wounded man sitting upon the ground waving his cap and cheering with the rest. Until nightfall, brigade after brigade charged across that field of death, to the dead-line, only to suffer disaster and defeat.

I see a regiment charging up the slope towards the stone wall opposite the Stephens' house. A large white dog is capering and leaping ahead of the column. My eyes follow another brigade advancing across the plain. They are veterans. The line keeps well dressed, but the men are bending as low as they can travel, and the color-bearers trailing their flags on the ground. Those heroic men are trying to avoid the Confederate bullets, but many in the ranks never took part in another fight. Here comes a regiment charging right towards us, advancing as orderly as if on dress parade. The cool conduct of their Colonel attracted the attention of a few, and some cried out:

"That's the way for a Colonel to bring in his men."

Some of the boys were jolly and laughing when they passed us, in close column, by the blacksmith shop, out of sight. See! some of them are already returning—I mean those that are wounded—to secure shelter along with us in front of the building. Two stalwart fellows came around the corner, dragging their dying Colonel riddled with bullets. That regiment must have been literally cut to pieces . . . .

A bullet crashed through the shop, throwing a splinter into the face of a man standing near. He cursed in hot anger and left the spot. From the blacksmith shop I hurriedly returned along the firing line to the red brick house, near which we opened fire in the assault . . . . General Kimball's brigade held its position at the firing-line until relieved, but even then the men could not safely retire. The only alternative was to lie at full length upon the ground, skulk into or behind neighboring buildings, or, at much greater risk of being shot down, withdraw to the rear. While at the brick house, looking around about me upon the awful scene of carnage, a bullet grazed my head. I watched a brigade charge up the slope, close to our left, but the brave men, unable to withstand the withering fire, soon fell back in disorder, followed by soldiers who had been at the dead-line since the first attack by Kimball's men. With a number of others, in the mixed throng collected in front of the brick building, the writer withdrew from the field. All the way down the slope to the edge of the town I saw my fellow-soldiers dropping on every side, in their effort to get out of the reach of the murderous fire from the Confederate infantry securely entrenched behind the long stone wall and the batteries on the heights. I saw a shell explode, close to the heels of a large man fleeing for his life. He was blown clear from the ground, falling in a heap, frightfully mangled. A little further on, another unfortunate fellow was lying on the ground, in a violent death struggle. At the edge of the town, two men were helping off the field a badly-wounded comrade, who was cursing in a frenzy of anger and vowing vengeance upon the rebels. A couple of stretcher carriers were carrying to the hospital a man with both legs shot away. It was a sickening sight. Scenes such as I have described made a lasting impression upon my memory.

*Benjamin Borton,*
*"On the Parallels"*

THE GROUND BETWEEN FREDERICKSBURG AND MARYE'S HEIGHTS.

(BL)

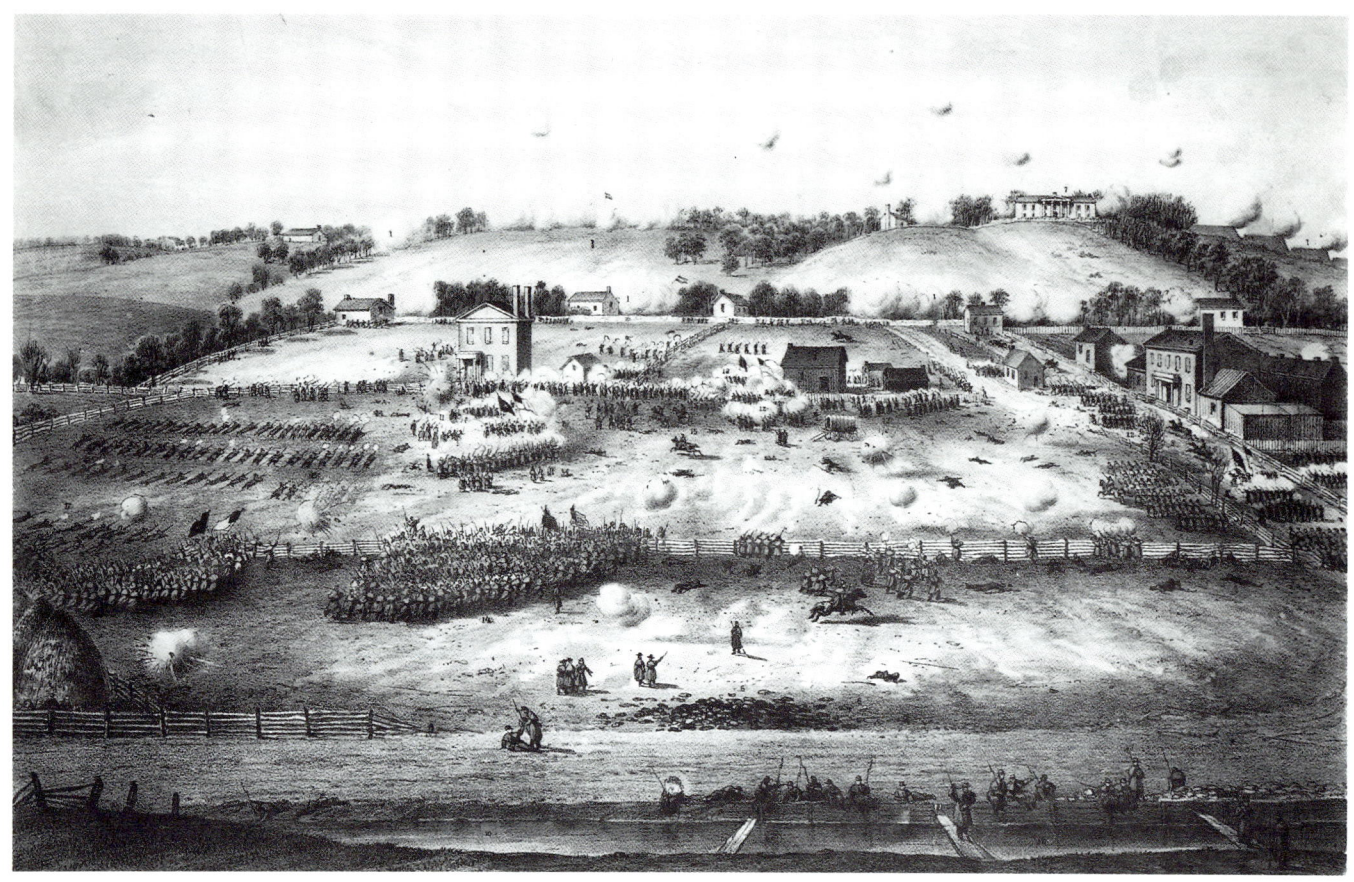

NATHAN KIMBALL'S BRIGADE WAS THE FIRST TO ATTACK MARYE'S HEIGHTS. DISREGARDING THE FIRE OF CONFEDERATE GUNS, KIMBALL'S MEN ADVANCED STEADILY TO WITHIN 60 YARDS OF THE STONE WALL. THEY COULD GO NO FURTHER.

(ANNE S. K. BROWN MILITARY COLLECTION, BROWN UNIVERSITY)

to mingle with Kimball's in the meager cover of that last shallow swale. About then a bullet snatched General Kimball's right leg from under him.

French's third brigade stormed over the rise a few minutes later, but the halt to maintain parade-ground intervals broke the momentum of those three regiments as well, and they finally plodded forward and shouldered into line with their predecessors. They knelt or lay in the muddy swale or hid behind the cluster of buildings in the fork of Hanover Street and the Telegraph Road, shooting ineffectually at the heights above them. Most of their rounds scattered into the embankment behind the Southern riflemen, whose eyes and muzzles alone peered over the stone wall, presenting a long, bright blade of fire that flayed the fat Federal line. French's assault was over.

## HANCOCK'S ATTACK, AND HOWARD'S

Next came Winfield Scott Hancock, with one of the best divisions in the Army of the Potomac. Hancock likewise threw his five thousand men at the wall in three waves. His first brigade rolled over French's stalled line, surging toward the still blue bodies that marked the limit of Kimball's farthest advance, sixty yards from the wall. There it stopped, though, and began creeping slowly backward as men shrank involuntarily from the withering fire. Behind them came the Irish Brigade, some twelve hundred strong, but neither could these veterans close the deadly gap between the lines; by day's end nearly five hundred of them had been shot.

Hancock's last brigade burst through the gaggle of survivors, losing much of its cohesion in the process, and sprinted for-

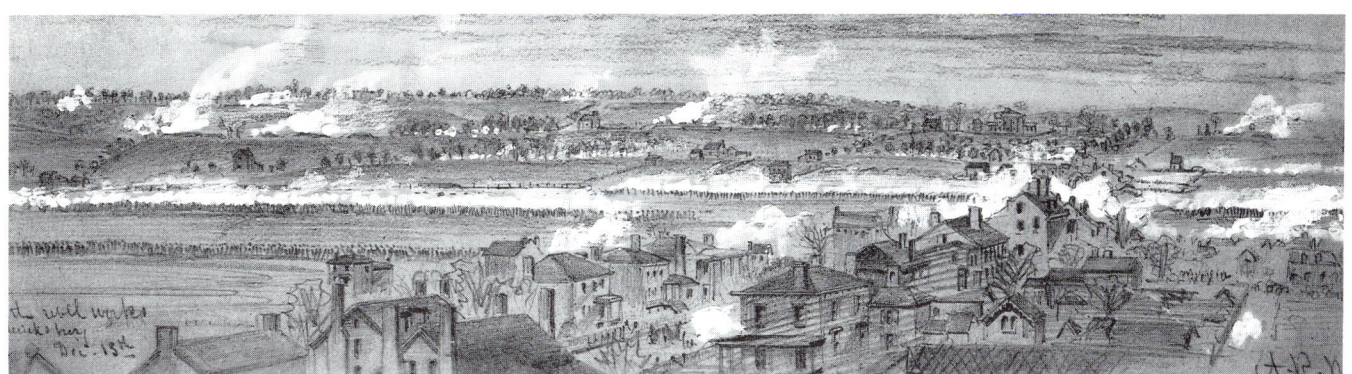

UNION TROOPS ATTACKING MARYE'S HEIGHTS, AS SEEN BY ARTIST ALFRED WAUD FROM A STEEPLE IN TOWN.
(LC)

ward past the earlier casualties. Parts of these six regiments came within shouting distance of the Telegraph Road, and individuals ventured closer still, but not in sufficient numbers to threaten the Confederate infantry. A deflected piece of shell bowled over the colonel of the 5th New Hampshire just beyond the millrace bluff. His men finished the assault under their major, who lifted his sword over his head and disappeared into the smoke before the stone wall, followed by half a dozen of his most

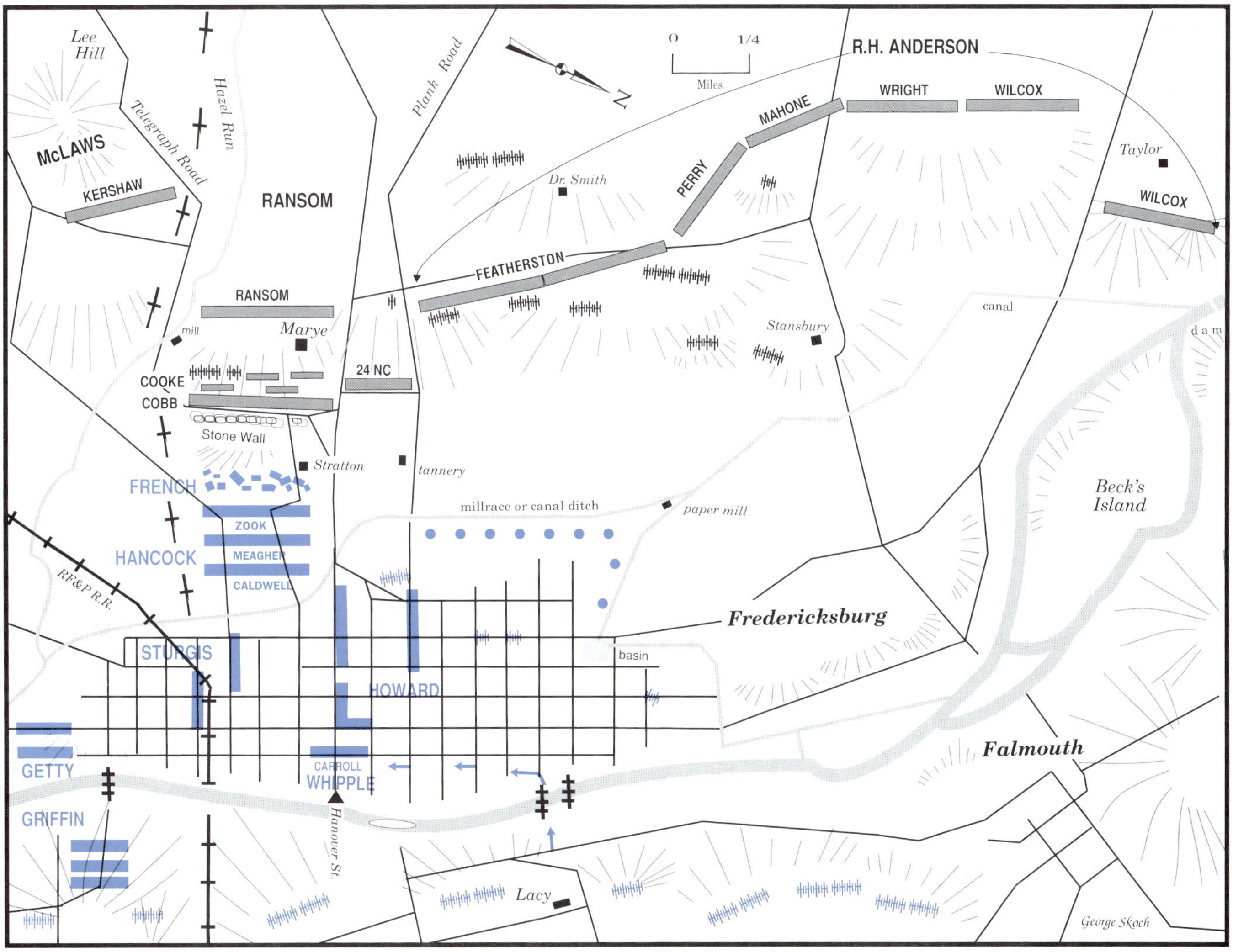

*HANCOCK GOES TO FRENCH'S SUPPORT: DECEMBER 13, 1 P.M.–2 P.M.*
*As French's attack falters, Couch sends Hancock's division forward to support it, but Hancock is likewise repulsed. Howard's division then files toward the front, hoping to outflank the Confederate defenders behind the stone wall while Sturgis advances to shore up Couch's endangered left flank. Meanwhile, part of Cooke's brigade joins Cobb's men in the Sunken Road.*

DARIUS COUCH
(BL)

intrepid soldiers. None of them came back, and that major may have been the officer whose body fell only thirty paces from the wall. "On all sides," wrote the wounded New Hampshire colonel, "men fell like grass before the scythe." Southern fire leveled 60 percent of his regiment.

From the courthouse cupola, Darius Couch watched the repulse of his first two divisions. As each brigade resolutely advanced into the face of Southern rifles, he wrote, it would "melt like snow coming down on warm ground." He soon realized that the Confederate line could not be broken at that point. Oliver O. Howard, the one-armed brigadier general who commanded Couch's remaining division, stood with him in the cupola. Just before one o'clock Couch ordered Howard to sidle farther to the right and attack the stone wall at the northern end, where he might be able to flank the riflemen hiding behind it. Simultaneously Couch sent couriers up to Hancock and French with orders to storm the wall, but those two appealed to Couch for reinforcements: between casualties and the stragglers who drifted away from the front by scores, the firing line was growing dangerously thin. Couch therefore canceled

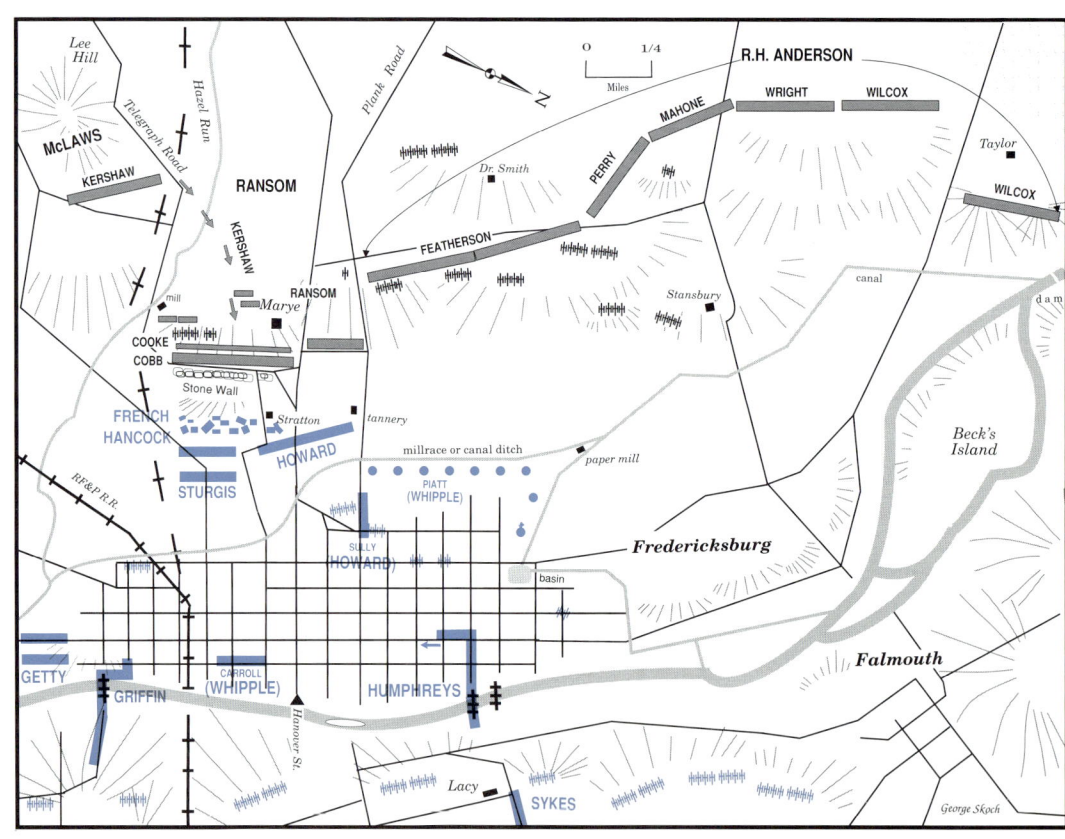

*STURGIS AND HOWARD ATTACK: DECEMBER 13, 2 P.M.-3 P.M.*
Sturgis advances in an effort to shore up Couch's left flank, while Howard attacks with two brigades astride Hanover Street. Ransom's brigade joins the fighting on the heights, while Kershaw's remaining regiments move down the Telegraph Road toward the front.

Howard's earlier orders and instructed him to go to Hancock's aid. Howard threw one brigade in behind Hancock, south of Hanover Street, and pushed another into the empty ground north of Hanover Street. He kept his last brigade just behind, on the outskirts of town.

For all the frustration of the Federal generals, Robert E. Lee feared that the mounting pressure in front of Marye's Heights might carry his line, but Longstreet assured him he could hold the stone wall. Two regiments of North Carolinians, exposed on the open hillside without rifle pits, plunged down into the Sunken Road to support the Georgians, whose General Cobb had fallen—within sight of the house where his parents were married—with shrapnel in his leg. He bled to death after being carried to the rear, but his men stood firm: during the whole fight his brigade suffered fewer casualties than some of the dozens of Union regiments that were hurled against the wall.

THOMAS R. R. COBB

(BL)

## STURGIS'S ASSAULT

Orlando B. Willcox waited at the lower end of town with the Federal Ninth Corps. Willcox had seen no progress on the center or right, and he mistook the movement of the two North Carolina regiments for an attack on Couch's left, so he sent forward Samuel Sturgis's division, one brigade at a time. Like those that went before, the first brigade met artillery fire the instant it emerged from the city. Green recruits in a new regiment gasped when a shell took one man's head off, showering them with jets of blood. Another shell exploded directly in front of a Massachusetts regiment, knocking down the whole color guard except the sergeant who carried Old Glory; after the blast he still stood, dazed and helpless in the acrid sulphur haze, clasping the flag to his breast with the bleeding stumps of his forearms. The man who took the staff from the handless sergeant was himself killed in a few moments, as was the one who took it from him.

His first brigade failed to gain any ground, so Sturgis swung his second one even farther to the left, increasing the length of open ground it would have to cover and bringing it within range of guns along the Confederate center. Beyond the railroad tracks sat a knoll cloven for another set of tracks that had never been finished, and when the front rank reached that cut it tumbled in. There it stayed in apparent safety, but the cut pointed like an arrow toward General Lee's command post, where squatted a 30-pounder Parrott rifle. This long-range gun started tossing shells into the cut, and frantic Union officers pushed, ordered, and begged their men to abandon that false refuge. The second rank

*Another shell exploded directly in front of a Massachusetts regiment, knocking down the whole color guard except the sergeant who carried Old Glory...*

ANDREW HUMPHREYS LED HIS PENNSYLVANIA DIVISION AGAINST THE WALL IN ONE OF THE FINAL ATTACKS OF THE DAY. ALTHOUGH APPROACHING TO WITHIN ONE HUNDRED YARDS OF THE WALL, HUMPHREYS WAS DRIVEN BACK, ADDING AN ADDITIONAL 1,000 NAMES TO THE MOUNTING CASUALTY ROLLS. (LC)

also fell into that trap, and Longstreet's artillery chief positioned a battery of Napoleons to rake the man-made ravine. Finally the shelling drove the last of Sturgis's men out, and they pressed on toward the stone wall. A few regiments in this second brigade did manage to work their way around the bend in the Telegraph Road, technically flanking the Georgians and Carolinians in the Sunken Road, but the steep slope neutralized their firepower.

## BURNSIDE ORDERS FRANKLIN TO TRY AGAIN

By now two o'clock had come and gone. It was at about this time that Burnside learned of Franklin's failure, ascribing it to a feeble effort. Convinced the Confederates had been shaken and that they might have shifted some of their strength to Franklin's front, Burnside decided to forgo fancy military tactics and simply hit both wings of Lee's army with everything he had, reverting to his plan of December 11. He directed Franklin to marshal his entire force for a direct assault on Jackson—which Franklin had already made, contrary to Burnside's intentions—and he ordered Hooker to pound Marye's Heights once again.

Franklin was in no mood to assault that wooded ridge again, for David Birney had just finished throwing back Jackson's counterattack. Franklin responded that he would do his best, yet most of his considerable strength remained idle. Hooker rode into Fredericksburg and conferred with Couch, who wanted to make a stab on the far right, where he had originally intended Howard to strike. Couch believed such an assault would work if Hooker used some of the four divisions he had left, but Hooker doubted whether the heights could be carried at all. He sent an aide to Burnside with that opinion, but the commanding general insisted that he cooperate. At that Hooker turned away from Couch and rode personally to general headquarters to persuade

Burnside the attack should be called off. Meanwhile, one of his divisions fell into the fight behind the mass of mixed commands on the plain beyond the city.

At 3:40 P.M. two officers on either end of Burnside's line scribbled exaggerated descriptions of the situation before them. On the left, General Hardie jotted down Franklin's pessimistic assessment of his own plight: two of his divisions were broken down, he said, and all the rest (but one) were engaged. Hardie promised that Franklin would make an attack if he could, but his message lacked enthusiasm. At the same instant, on the right, one of Hooker's corps commanders relayed an incorrect report that Couch had carried Marye's Heights and wanted more support. Hooker had found Burnside only a few moments before, and Burnside decided to go for broke. He told Hooker to go back into the city and press his attack, fully expecting that Franklin would do the same.

## Humphreys Attacks

The December sun drooped near the crest of Marye's Heights as Hooker reentered Fredericksburg and directed Andrew A. Humphreys to lead his division against the stone wall. Humphreys—a short, graying brigadier who had attended West Point with Robert E. Lee—commanded two brigades of Pennsylvanians, most of whom were nine-month militiamen. None of his eight regiments had ever seen action before.

Humphreys hurried ahead of his foremost brigade as it trotted out of town into the same maelstrom that had tattered earlier divisions. Over the bridges they marched, filing to the right into columns of assault under the shelter of the millrace bluff. Humphreys tried to work his formation to the right, to flank that part of the Confederate line that had been thrown forward to the stone wall salient, but the millrace and canal barred their passage there. The guidons on the right of Humphreys's line did not pass beyond William Street. In front sprawled Howard's prone survivors, pinned behind their own shallow terrace, but this stretch of the Union front offered the least congestion: a short way to the left, the refuse of broken divisions lay six or eight brigades deep.

Up at the stone wall, Joseph Kershaw had succeeded the dying Cobb, and Kershaw's South Carolina brigade had reinforced Cobb's Georgians. Confederate marksmen filled the Sunken Road, eagerly awaiting new targets though their ranks

JOSEPH HOOKER

(USAMHI)

*In front sprawled Howard's prone survivors, pinned behind their own shallow terrace, but this stretch of the Union front offered the least congestion: a short way to the left, the refuse of broken divisions lay six or eight brigades deep.*

CONFEDERATES IN THE
SUNKEN ROAD

(BL)

had jumbled as hopelessly as those of the Yankees who lay before them. Kershaw's brigade once included a lieutenant named A. W. Burnside—one of the Federal commander's South Carolina cousins.

General Humphreys kneed his horse and pointed his sword, leading his first two thousand rifles over the bluff in double lines of two regiments each. They jogged bravely forward with canister ripping their ranks, but the first deafening crash of musketry struck them just as they reached Howard's frayed line and most of them dove to the ground. Humphreys galloped frantically about, exposing himself recklessly as he tried to shout above the din. With a herculean effort he convinced his hapless novitiates to stand up in the deadly storm and dress ranks for a bayonet charge.

Thousands of bullets had thinned the brigade fearfully, though, and those who dared to press forward were too few to challenge the wall. A battery to their right belched canister the length of their line, and the musketry only intensified until they turned back to the swale.

His horse had been killed under him, but the undaunted Humphreys borrowed a courier's mount and rode back to the bluff, where he gave his other brigade a hasty lesson in military tactics. If they did not stop to fire, he told them, but merely sprinted past the prone brigades toward the wall, they could leap in among the enemy and drive them off with the bayonet before they lost too many men. The promiscuous masses behind them would rise up and follow, and the day would be won. That sort of thinking had cost the British dearly at Bunker Hill, and the extra range of rifled muskets only worsened the odds, but such brutal tricks still worked now and then: a different brigade led by the same man who commanded this one, Erastus B. Tyler, had successfully charged another stone wall at Kernstown the previous March, giving Stonewall Jackson his only defeat.

Once again Humphreys posted himself alongside the brigade commander and spurred his horse over the bluff, followed by 2,200 Pennsylvanians.

They, too, leaned resolutely into the firestorm, but as they neared the firing line their comrades shouted that it was no

ANDREW A. HUMPHREYS

(BL)

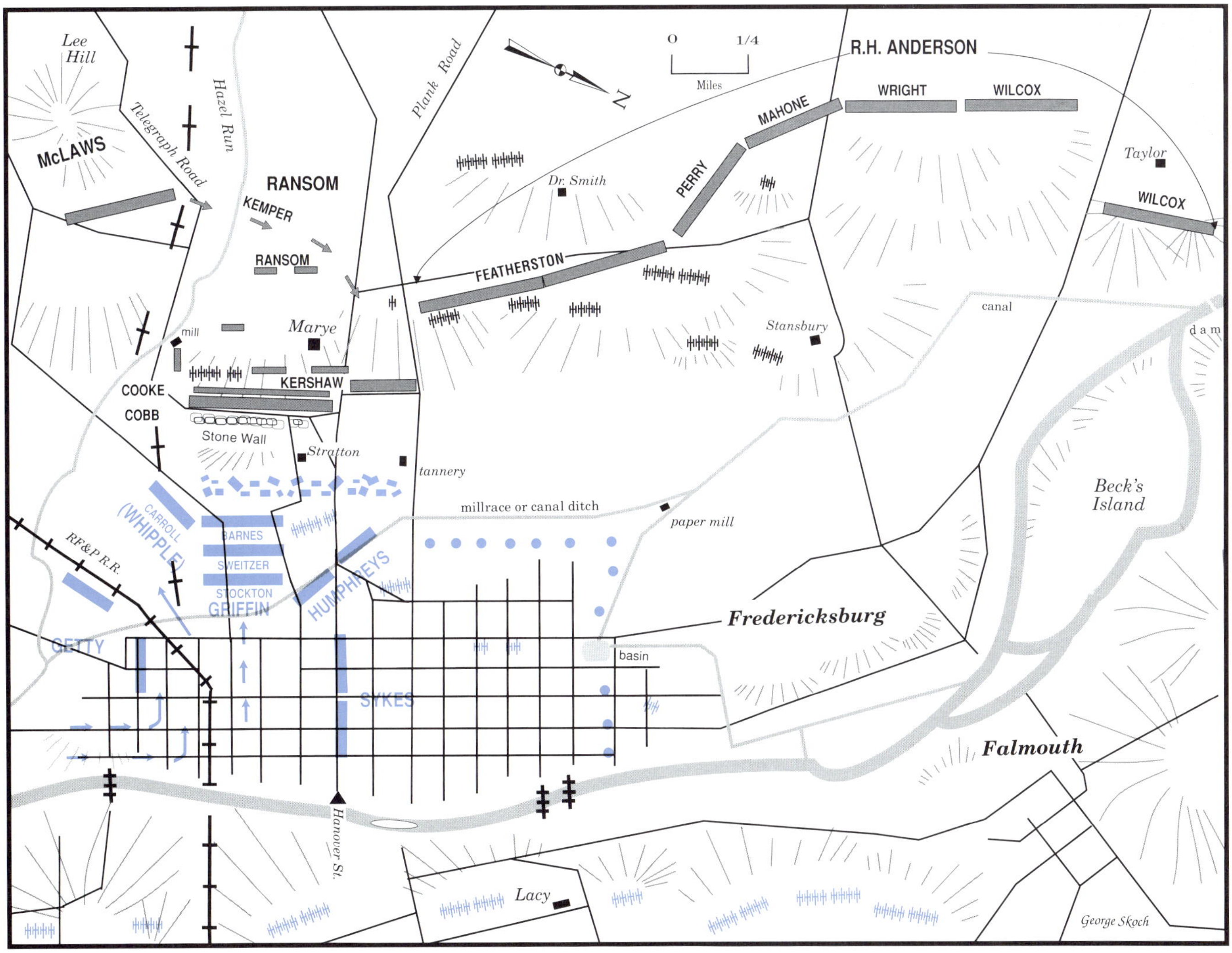

*GRIFFIN GOES IN: DECEMBER 13, 3 P.M.– 5 P.M.*

*In an effort to weaken the Confederate line, Couch orders Hazard's battery to the front to shell Marye's Heights at close range, where it is soon joined by Frank's battery. Griffin meanwhile attacks the stone wall head-on, supported on his left by Carroll's brigade of Whipple's division. Getty and Humphreys move into position to join the assault. On the Confederate side, two of Kershaw's regiments, the 3rd and 7th South Carolina, take position on the hillcrest near the Marye house, while Kemper's brigade hurries forward from Lee's Hill to reinforce the 24th Georgia. The Washington Artillery runs out of ammunition on Marye's Heights and is replaced by guns of Alexander's battalion.*

use, waving them down, begging them to take cover, and tugging at their cuffs and coattails. Enough of the column succumbed to these pleas to shatter the collective momentum. Those brave enough to surmount that last deadly little shelf quickly fell or turned back. Humphreys lost his second horse, mounted a third, and motioned the brigade back to the millrace bluff to consolidate its thinned and jumbled formation.

"No campaign in the world ever saw a more gallant advance than Humphreys's men made there," said Joe Hooker.

*Samuel Sturgis, whose division lay directly beneath the muzzles of Cobb's and Kershaw's muskets, sent back a note at dark saying "our men only 80 paces from the crest & holding on like hell."*

## GETTY'S ASSAULT

At the southern end of town Orlando Willcox hoped to draw some of the pressure off Humphreys by throwing George Getty's division at the bend in the Telegraph Road. Most of Getty's first brigade was also new to combat—one regiment had reached the army only four days previously. Even the officers advanced reluctantly, at least one of them willing the sun to sink and end the battle.

The horizon did blaze briefly orange through the sulphurous haze as they approached Marye's Heights, but in the twilight Southern gunners could still see well enough to rake the oncoming ranks after they passed the railroad cut. When the bright new flags veered diagonally toward the Sunken Road, the Georgians and Carolinians turned to greet them. Canister scattered the left flank of this column, rifles flamed at it from the front, and when nervous Federals near the millrace angled an errant volley into their backs the brigade melted and drained to the rear.

The second brigade of Getty's division did not attack, nor did Humphreys renew his assault. As these last valiant endeavors had moved forward, Burnside received Franklin's 4:30 announcement that he had not found time to arrange an assault. In the two hours since Franklin had claimed he would "do his best" to cooperate with them, however, his counterparts on the right wing had thrown in three fresh divisions and launched three separate attacks. Between the darkness and Franklin's lethargy, Burnside knew he could do nothing more. The last uncommitted division on the right wing, U.S. Regulars under Brigadier General George Sykes, covered the withdrawal of Humphreys's battered division, and when the fighting ended Sykes counted more casualties from his defensive maneuver than Abner Doubleday suffered in his nominal support of Meade's attack. In further testimony to the poverty of Franklin's efforts, his entire Sixth Corps lost fewer men than ten of the seventeen brigades that charged the stone wall.

Despite the day's failures and a gloomy message from officers across the river, who predicted that infantry alone could never carry Marye's Heights, Burnside remained hopeful. Samuel Sturgis, whose division lay directly beneath the muzzles of the Confederate muskets, sent back a note at dark saying "our men only 80 paces from the crest & holding on like hell." Headquarters burned with determination—and in some cases with confidence—that evening, and Burnside stayed awake to plan another double assault to polish off the Confederates the next day.

That same night Lee made further preparations for the assault he thought

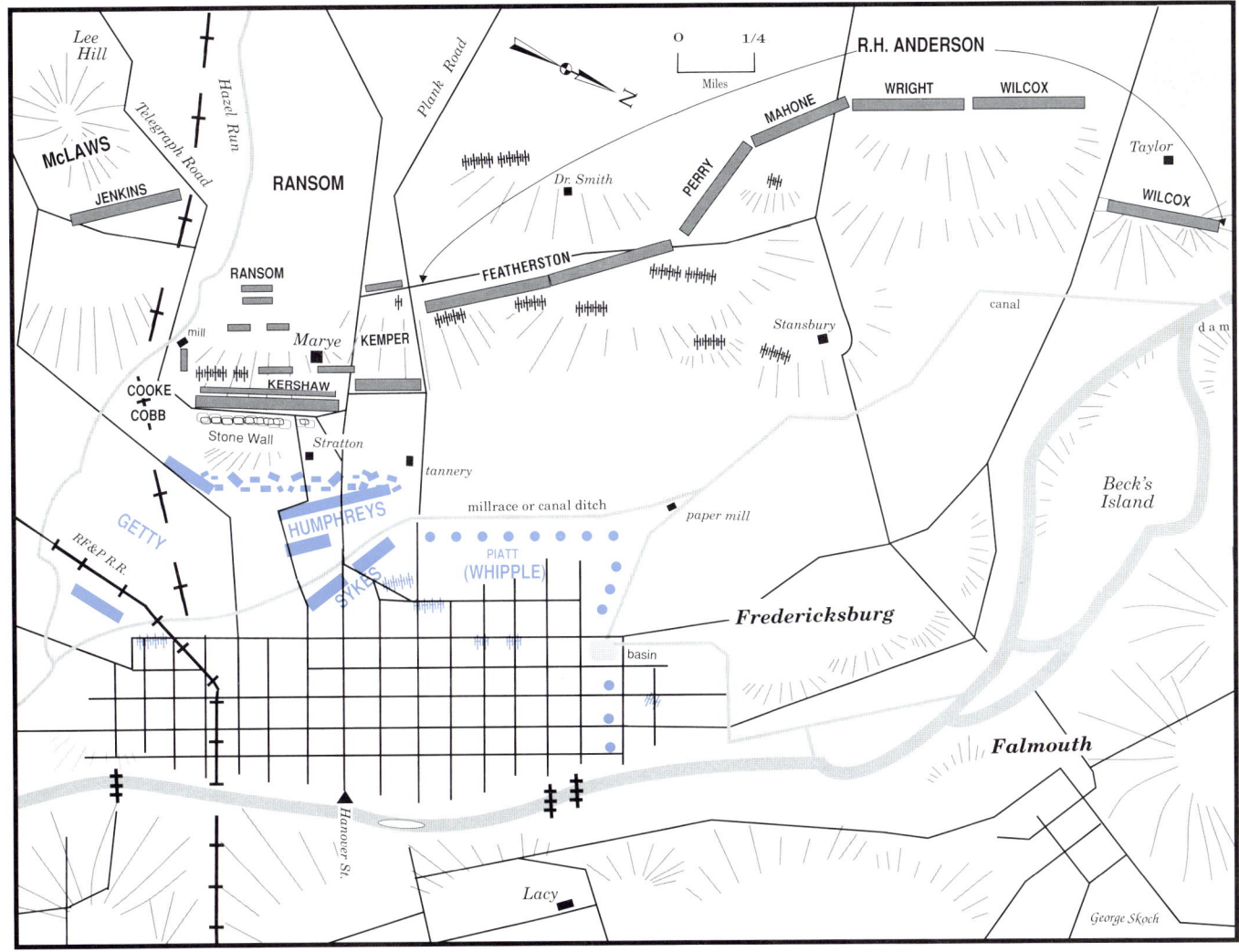

**HUMPHREYS AND HAWKINS ATTACK: DECEMBER 13, 5 P.M.–6 P.M.**
With sunlight fast disappearing, Humphreys's division advances past the Stratton House to attack the stone wall. Although approaching within 50 yards of the wall, it is repulsed by the Confederates, who now stand six ranks deep in the Sunken Road. Getty attacks the southern end of the wall at dark with Hawkins's brigade, leaving Harland in reserve back at the railroad. Sykes's division takes position along the millrace from which it will advance at 11 P.M. to relieve Humphreys's division at the front.

likely. All along the Confederate line infantrymen pieced together little breastworks. Now that Lee knew Burnside meant business in front of Marye's Heights he directed his artillerymen to spend the night strengthening the lunettes for their guns: if the heights had been strong on December 13, they would be impregnable on December 14.

While the Confederates worked atop Marye's Heights, Union wounded below them wailed piteously. Bitterly cold air plagued them as well as thirst and pain, but few of them could be evacuated because the enemy lay so close. Their cries carried across the river, even to Burnside's headquarters.

## SECOND THOUGHTS

Burnside recognized that piecemeal attacks would not be strong enough to carry Marye's Heights, and he already suspected Franklin had not supported him enthusiastically enough, but today he planned for a grand assault on either side.

Burnside intended to lead his old Ninth Corps against the stone wall personally, for he remained extremely popular with these men and they might be expected to follow him more zealously than someone else: morale could mean the difference between success and failure.

Most of the generals in the Army of the Potomac doubted any assault on the stone wall could succeed. When Burnside called a conference the next morning General Sumner revealed the universal skepticism. Burnside might have questioned the motives of other officers, many of whom remained true to McClellan, but he could not discount the loyal old Sumner; when the morning fog cleared and Burnside turned his binoculars on the strengthened Confederate line, he decided to cancel the attack.

Discussion then turned to how (and whether) to hold the town. Some, Darius Couch among them, argued that morale would plummet after so great a loss if the army could not even embrace Fredericksburg as a prize. More traditional strategists feared that the gray hordes might surge down from the heights and drive the beaten army into the river. For the moment, Burnside determined to hold the ground he had won.

Skirmish fire rattled along both fronts throughout the morning of December 14. In front of Marye's Heights Union sharpshooters sniped away from the shelter of the few buildings on the plain. The rest of the Federal pickets hugged the cold earth, taking futile, dangerous potshots at the stone wall and listening to the pleas of their own wounded. That pitiful chorus carried all the louder into Confederate lines, though, affecting one South Carolina sergeant in particular. Burdening himself with all the canteens he could manage,

Richard Kirkland bounded over the stone wall and started toward the windrows of suffering Yankees.

RICHARD R. KIRKLAND
(CAROLINIANA COLLECTION, UNIVERSITY OF SOUTH CAROLINA)

Sykes's division of Regulars watched from within easy rifle range, but the lone Southron reached the first wounded man unhurt. Once his mission became clear, picket fire dropped off entirely, and Kirkland ranged along the front in perfect safety, dispensing water and sympathy.

That night Longstreet's men resumed work on their fortifications while Burnside pulled Sykes back nearer the city. The next day the standoff continued, with Hooker commanding the defense of the city. Hooker had already lobbied for the evacuation of all but a couple of divisions: with so many troops crowded into the narrow streets he feared Confederate artillery could wreak some real havoc here, besides which the buildings still offered refuge to hundreds of demoralized stragglers. If Burnside was not going to make another assault,

# ON THE PICKET LINE AT FREDERICKSBURG

On the evening of December 14th, General Doubleday wanted our regiment (the 2d Wisconsin) to go on picket and make an effort to stop the firing upon the picket-line, for the shots of the Confederates covered the whole field, and no one could get any rest. We had not been in the picket-line more than twenty minutes before we made a bargain with the "Rebs," and the firing ceased, and neither they nor ourselves pretended to keep under cover. But at daylight the 24th Michigan came to relieve us. Before they were fairly in line they opened fire upon the Confederates without the warning we had agreed to give. We yelled lustily, but the rattle of musketry drowned the sound, and many a confiding enemy was hit. This irritated the Confederates, who opened a savage fire, and the 24th Michigan were put upon their good behavior; it was with difficulty a general engagement was prevented. All that day, until about 4 o'clock, the picket-firing was intense; it was abruptly ended by a Confederate challenging a 6th Wisconsin man to a fist-fight in the middle of the turnpike. The combatants got the attention of both picket-lines, who declared the fight a "draw." They ended the matter with a coffee and tobacco trade and an agreement to do no more firing at picket-line, unless an advance should be ordered.

*George E. Smith, "In the Ranks at Fredericksburg"*

GENERAL FRANKLIN MADE HIS HEADQUARTERS ON THE GROUNDS OF ARTHUR BERNARD'S HOUSE, "MANNSFIELD." UNION SOLDIERS VANDALIZED THE STRUCTURE IN DECEMBER, 1862, AND CARELESS CONFEDERATE PICKETS SET IT ON FIRE THE FOLLOWING APRIL. BY WAR'S END, THE HOUSE, LIKE SO MANY OTHERS IN THE FREDERICKSBURG AREA, WAS A RUIN. (BL)

*That night, with tears of frustration in his eyes, Burnside gave orders for a careful withdrawal.*

Hooker felt that the bulk of the right wing ought to march back to Falmouth. He also hinted at a complete evacuation on the morning of the 15th, but Burnside had already decided to bring his whole army back. That night, with tears of frustration in his eyes, Burnside gave orders for a careful withdrawal.

## The Withdrawal

Retreating across a river in the immediate presence of an enemy is perhaps the most dangerous operation a general can conduct, but Burnside extricated his army unnoticed. Artillery crossed first, beginning at dusk. Behind a thick cordon of pickets the infantry started over next, the echo of their footsteps muffled by a cold, heavy rain. By four o'clock in the morning all of Franklin's men stood safely on the left bank, and engineers began dismantling not only his bridges but two of those in front of Fredericksburg.

Provost details scoured the city for stragglers, flushing scores of them out of houses and cellars. A brigade of Regulars backpedaled toward the river as rear guard. When that last brigade reached the riverbank its nervous officers found their assigned bridge taken up. After some frantic consultation they spotted another one still intact a few blocks away and marched their men toward it just as the gray skies lightened for another dreary day. Last of all came the provost guards, herding platoons of stragglers whom they had to ferry over in loose pontoon boats. By full daylight only the final fragments of the bridges remained.

When the fog burned away the Confederates finally discovered the flight, and a couple of Kershaw's regiments spilled into the city to picket the waterfront. They found a few more lingering looters. At least one returning citizen caught a Pennsylvanian asleep in his cellar, prodding him toward an officer at the point of his own bayonet.

THE BATTLE LEFT FEW HOMES IN FREDERICKSBURG UNSCARRED. ONE HOUSE WAS HIT BY NO LESS THAN 132 CANNONBALLS.

(USAMHI)

The town lay ruined in some quarters, and nearly every house bore the scars of shell, round shot, or bullets. Three brothers who had grown up in Fredericksburg took leave of their companies long enough to examine the old family home, finding the library rifled. They tracked the course of one shell through the house, and counted the pockmarks on the brick walls. For all the damage, they considered themselves lucky. Had they proceeded to the garret they might have felt more fortunate still, for there lay the body of a Yankee who had been killed while pecking away at the distant Confederate works.

Hundreds of Union dead still lay where they had fallen in front of Marye's Heights. When the sun next emerged, the slope appeared blue with their clothing. Burnside made arrangements for a burial party to cross over the next day and hack mass graves out of the crusty December clay. Once assured the Yankees were gone, however, poorly clad Southerners scurried out in the darkness to strip the wool uniforms from bodies that would no longer need them, and when Federal sextons reached the heights on December 17 they found the place gleaming fishbelly-white with naked corpses. Over the next two days they counted 918 bodies, only five of which they could identify as officers. For two days their picks and shovels rang, and many a hero like the New Hampshire major found an anonymous grave.

Of the 12,653 total Union casualties, more than sixty percent had fallen before the stone wall. That was more men than McClellan had lost at Antietam, and

AFTER THE BATTLE, UNION BURIAL PARTIES RECROSSED THE RIVER UNDER A FLAG OF TRUCE. MANY OF THE DEAD HAD BEEN STRIPPED OF THEIR CLOTHING BY THE CONFEDERATES AND LAY NAKED ON THE COLD GROUND.

(LC)

Burnside had not even held the field. Lee had suffered fewer than 5400 casualties.

The failure and the disproportionate loss demoralized Northern soldiers and civilians alike. After General Sumner dissuaded him from resigning on December 15, Burnside exclaimed, "No man can ever know what this has cost me." At an inspection on Christmas Eve, the decimated Irish Brigade refused to cheer him until Sumner discreetly ordered them to do so. Newspaper editors criticized the administration for urging a hasty move against the enemy, but Burnside responded directly, publicly assuming all responsibility for the disaster. Many of his subordinate generals—particularly Franklin, who harbored a more personal motive—pounced upon this admission and began slandering their commander openly.

FIVE WEEKS AFTER THE BATTLE OF FREDERICKSBURG, BURNSIDE LED THE ARMY OF THE POTOMAC UPRIVER IN A WINTER OFFENSIVE KNOWN AS THE "MUD MARCH." BAD WEATHER THWARTED BURNSIDE'S PLANS AND LED TO HIS DISMISSAL AS ARMY COMMANDER.

(LC)

## DENOUEMENT

Unlike George McClellan might have, Burnside quickly recovered after the defeat. Political pressure (and General Halleck) called for a winter campaign, despite the obvious impediments it posed for the aggressor. Burnside proposed a flanking maneuver and issued orders for the movement, but on the eve of the offensive General Franklin gave the two senior generals in one of his divisions leave to visit President Lincoln and discourage him about the operation. Though he obviously disapproved of this intrigue, the president did direct Burnside to cancel his orders, and the general sailed up to Washington to discuss his obstructionist subordinates. They came to no conclusion, though, and Burnside went back to the army.